Lean the f*ck Out

How to Aim Lower + Get Less Done + Find Your Happiness

Talia Argondezzi

CASTLE POINT BOOKS
NEW YORK

To Susan and Charles,
who worked way too hard
but still managed to find
themselves some happiness

. . . .

www.castlepointbooks.com

The Castle Point Books trademark is owned by
Castle Point Publishing, LLC.
Castle Point books are published and distributed by
St. Martin's Publishing Group.

ISBN 978-1-250-28708-3 (hardcover)
ISBN 978-1-250-28709-0 (ebook)

Design by Tara Long
Composition by Noora Cox
Edited by Aimee Chase

Our books may be purchased in bulk for promotional,
educational, or business use.

Please contact your local bookseller or the Macmillan Corporate
and Premium Sales Department at 1-800-221-7945, extension
5442, or by email at MacmillanSpecialMarkets@macmillan.com.

First Edition: 2023

10 9 8 7 6 5 4 3 2 1

Contents

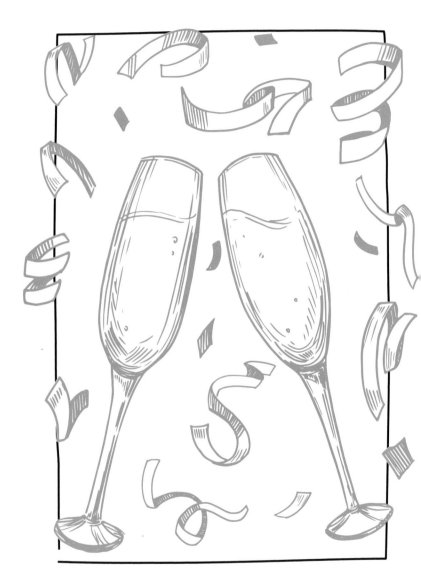

A Joyful
→ *no-bullshit* ←
Manifesto

Benjamin Franklin, the famous statesman and inventor who, according to Wikipedia, apparently never became U.S. president, started every morning with a meditation: What good will I do today? And every night, after taking off his weird, white, eighteenth-century wig and polishing his bifocals (which he invented) and drinking his eighteenth-century sleepy-time tea or whatever, he dozed off with another meditation: What good did I do today? This is according to his autobiography, which was mostly bullshit, but still, there were some promising ideas in there.

I, on the other hand, sometimes find myself starting the day with the panicked scream, "Shit! I have so much to do today!" and end the evening lying in bed scolding myself, "Damn, you dummy, you didn't get anything done today!" In other words, Ben started his day by setting an intention and ended the day with a positive reflection. He was sort of an early life coach, and if I remember correctly, this self-encouragement seemed to work out for him. In contrast, a lot of us tend to start the day with worry and end the day with regret.

If you constantly feel like you have too much to do, and constantly feel like you "didn't get anything done," the problem might not be your personal productivity or lack thereof. The problem may be that you're holding yourself to an impossible standard.

This book is a supportive and bullshit-free manifesto for anyone who is doing way too fucking much.

And there are plenty of us out there. It's for married women, divorced men, stay-at-home parents, young and trying-too-hard workers, old and tired workers, young tired workers, working parents, moonlighters, household managers, emotional laborers. It's for statesmen, authors, inventors, publishers, entrepreneurs, diplomats—okay, those are all just descriptions of Ben Franklin, but for real, dude, give it a rest; you're doing too much. This book is for you too, bud.

It's for people who hear demands coming from all different directions—from our jobs both in the home and out, from spouses or lovers or kids, from parents and friends and coworkers—and as a result, who have become pretty self-demanding. We tend to feel pressure to perform a certain way, both professionally and personally. We often feel like we never have a break, and as a result, we rarely give ourselves a break.

This book is all about self-encouragement and taking a leap. Remind yourself that not every fucking thing is your personal responsibility.

Why not try something new and let yourself off the hook?

Wait,
Is There *Actual Advice*
in This Book?

Fuck yeah!

There's great stuff in self-help books, lots of times. And this is one of those times. (If anyone has ever shamed you for reading self-help, tell them to fuck off. Also, tell them to read a self-help book about how to stop being so damn mean.)

The main goal of this book is to make you chuckle, because I'm assuming you need to laugh more than you need to be told what to do.

However, in addition to being a humor writer, I'm also really fucking bossy and I know what it feels like to be doing too much and living too little. So, yeah, there's serious advice wrapped inside jokes in here.

That said, if you think self-help books are a little silly, you're also right. You heard me: Something can be good and helpful but also kind of silly.

The way I see it, even if it's written by a brilliant, credentialed psychologist/businessperson/surgeon or whatever who's led an impeccably perfect life and wants to show you how you can too, the "help" part of the self-help book operates more or less like astrology or fortune-telling. You might not literally believe the horoscope or fortune is true, but it gives you some starting point or a little nudge to reflect. Self-help books, like horoscopes, offer food for thought. And you can enjoy that food for thought however you like.

Giving you a menu of ideas about how life should be lived, and letting you pick the ones that intuitively feel right to you? That's what self-help books can do, even satirical self-help books written by a non-brilliant humorist who hasn't led a perfect life and has no credentials. (Actually, I do have a PhD, but it's in English, so I'm only technically qualified to help you interpret poetry.)

So yeah, this book has some real, honest-to-goodness tips about how to make your life better.

Specifically, how to make your life better by leaning the fuck out.

Is This Book *Only* for Women?

Kind of, yes. But mostly this book is for people with particular characteristics.

Here are some types of people who, regardless of gender, might need some help with leaning the fuck out. See if you find yourself in this list:

The Super-Apologizer. You apologize a lot, but then remember that you've been told not to apologize so much, and then feel guilty for apologizing so much, and then apologize for apologizing.

The Anger Swallower. You sometimes start a conversation angry at another person, but end it apologizing to that person, even though you still know you're right.

The Productivity Self-Flagellator. You start some days saying, "I have so much to do!" and then do stuff all day, but still end the day hating yourself because you "didn't get anything done today."

The Insomniac List-Maker. You sometimes have trouble falling asleep until you make a list of all the things you have to do the next day.

The Productivity Addict. You take more pleasure in checking things off your to-do list than in actually doing things.

The Bundle of Nerves. You had a panic attack when you read *Lean In*.

The Leisure Loser. When you find yourself in a rare moment when no one is asking you for anything, you think to yourself, "I should do something I enjoy right now!" but then realize you don't know what to do with yourself because you're so far removed from what you used to do when you actually chose how to spend your time.

If you found yourself on this list, it's time to let yourself off the hook and stop trying to do it all.

Where Do I *Begin*?

There's only one solution to the problem of doing too fucking much: Stop.

Stop vacuuming the shit out of your house. Stop cooking homemade meals when you are falling over tired. Stop taking on extra work at the office when you're very competent as is. Stop letting social media drain your energy and confidence—stop putting more effort into looking like you're having fun than actually having fun.

Start by stopping.

The purpose of *Lean the F*ck Out* is to help you:

☆ Underachieve more.

☆ Related: Achieve less.

☆ Aim lower.

☆ Get really bad at one thing.

☆ Then, get bad at a whole bunch of things.

☆ Let a few things slide.

☆ Once you've let a few things slide a bit, let them slide all the way off. Then let them go. Forever.

☆ Untangle your sense of self-worth from your belief that you've "accomplished" something in the eyes of your friends, your boss, your "followers," your mom, your judgy neighbor, etc.

☆ Feel happy about failing more, because you'll be leaving yourself time to actually have fun and enjoy life.

You definitely don't need any help doing and achieving. You've already achieved enough. You've already done too much.

Instead, you need help giving yourself a break. It's time to stop leaning in. You need some help leaning the fuck out.

The Main Principles of Leaning *the Fuck* Out

Principle 1 is simple:

Say "yes" less.

You know how people ask you to do shit all the time? Your new default answer is "no."

True, when push comes to shove, you're eventually going to have to do some things, both for yourself and for others.

But stop jumping up right away and doing it without even thinking.

> *Nike was talking to triathletes and NBA players when they said to Just Do It. The rest of us can just chill the fuck out on the couch.*

It's going to feel, many times, like you must do the task being requested, whatever it is. But I'm asking you to just *try* saying no. Try not doing it. See what happens.

Did your husband just ask you where his keys are? Wait a beat. He might actually find them on his own.

Shoot for the moon. Even if you miss, you'll end up among the stars.^

where you'll suffer a fiery death, combusting from traveling at the velocity required to exit the Earth's atmosphere

Did the boss ask for someone to volunteer to take notes at the meeting, and you don't really mind taking notes, and no one else is saying anything, and you're starting to get uncomfortable? Don't say anything. Don't volunteer to take those fucking notes. Just see what happens. Probably someone else will volunteer. Simply wait.

Are there a shit-ton of dishes in the sink? And it's looking gross? And it bothers you that it looks gross but it doesn't bother anybody else in your house? So, you're probably going to have to wash the dishes? Just *don't* do it. Let's find out what happens here. (I regret to inform you that if you live alone, you're going to have to wash those dishes eventually. But you see my point.)

The second principle here, which is just a logical extension of the first, is:

Only do what you really need or want to do.

Are you worried you don't have any idea what you really *want* to do? Don't worry, we'll cover that later in the book.

Our third principle is going to help you with the first and second. The third principle is:

Ask more questions.

First of all, of course you have to ask some questions about the task at hand. Important, heavy-hitting questions, like "Before you asked me to help you find your keys, did you look in all the places your keys usually are? Did you look in your jacket pocket?"

Questions like that are really going to help you say no to some requests.

But really, even more importantly, you have to ask some questions of yourself. Questions like "Wait, what do I actually *need* and *want* to do?"

Coming up against that question will lead you to the fourth principle:

Sort the stuff you love to do from all the shit you're expected to do.

Once you've stopped saying yes to everything and you've whittled your life down to what you really need to do and want to do, you might end up with a blessed (or terrifying?) amount of free time. Faced with free time, you might initially, instinctively fill it with the very menial, soul-crushing, unfulfilling garbage you are trying to escape in the first place, like jumping up to find your partner's keys or caving and washing your roommates' dishes.

And why is that?

Because a lot of us have become so accustomed to doing shit we don't want to do, that we actually start believing we like it.

For example, you might think, "I'm not washing these dishes for my family or roommates. I'm washing them because I love having a clean kitchen. The dirty dishes are bothering me. I'll feel better when they're clean. I'm actually doing this chore for myself."

Get a fucking grip, girl. You *think* you like washing dishes because you've been trained to think having a clean kitchen is your duty and because having washed the dishes gives you a sense of accomplishment. Even if you genuinely, in the depths of your soul, no bullshit, love washing dishes, think about the other things you could be doing with that time if you weren't washing dishes. Maybe composing a symphony. Or inventing a new product. Or calling a loved one you haven't spoken to in a while. If you're thinking, "But I don't know how to write music. I don't have any product ideas. I haven't talked to some friends in so long they'd be confused if I called them. I'll just wash these dishes," friend, you've been washing other people's dishes for too damn long. It takes a lot of leaning the fuck out to even discover what you like to do with your free time.

But also, I may have been shooting a little too high with examples of what to do with your freed-up non-dish-washing time. The fact is, you don't even need to be composing a fucking symphony or connecting with a long-lost friend every single second.

Your time is worthwhile even if you're not doing something "important" with it.

And that's the next principle.

Be okay with any level of productivity.

Here's how to do it:

- ☆ Let yourself watch *Real Housewives of [Location of Your Choice]* without feeling like you should be doing something else.

- ☆ Abolish the idea of "guilty pleasures" and only have pleasures.

- ☆ Abolish the idea of wasted time. Stare into space a while.

- ☆ Don't check anything off your to-do list all day. (Then throw away your to-do list and go back to principle 2: Only do what you really want to do.)

The point is not that you'll never "get things done" again. You can still get things done! If you want to! And if it makes sense for your life right then! The point, instead, is this: Before you get anything done, the first thing you need to get done is being okay with not getting some things done.

Which leads us to the final principle of leaning the fuck out:

Destroy your inner critic.

You may also have external critics. And although you can't legally destroy them (unfortunately), you should probably get them out of your life ASAP. They're not helping. Once you're rid of all those awful people, time to look at all the fucking bullshit you've internalized.

I once found myself apologizing for stopping at the gym on the way home from work. This sounded something like, "Sorry that on my way home from providing for our family, I'm going to take thirty minutes to exercise so I don't die young of heart disease." Is this impulse to apologize for doing very ordinary things for myself because I have some kind of abusive, demanding spouse who demands I'm home at a certain time? Nope. I'm married to a total peach.

I apologized because my inner critic is convinced that I need to be everywhere at all times so I can be everything to everyone.

That bitch is exhausting! (Our inner critic, I mean.)

Shut. Her. Down.

So, to review, here are the main ideas behind leaning the fuck out:

#1 Say "fuck you!" to saying yes to everything.

#2 Make time to do whatever the fuck you want to do. (Step 1: Actually consider what that might be.)

#3 Question others.

#4 Then question yourself—because you may be a little brainwashed.

#5 Be a B student for once in your life.

#6 Dropkick your inner critic right out the door.

It's pretty hard to do all those things, though. That's why you have this book as a guide!

Throw Your Sense of Who You *"Should"* Be into the Deepest Ocean

I'd like to introduce you to my Sense of Who I'm Supposed to Be. Let's call her . . . I don't know, Sage? Veronica?

**KEEP
CALM
AND
CARRY
~~ON.~~**

→ Tums—
In case the
"keeping calm" thing
isn't working

She has some name I'm not quite cool enough to pull off. She:

☆ excels at work and is noticed and promoted often.

☆ provides home-cooked healthy environmentally friendly nutritious food for every meal.

☆ lives in a stylish and neat house.

☆ always buys organic—or better yet, grows food and flowers in her backyard.

☆ looks effortlessly chic and fit and gorgeous all the time.

☆ never says anything awkward. How could she? She doesn't have any awkward thoughts.

☆ has a couple of precocious and well-behaved children in tow.

☆ displays all these assets online in a sincere, authentic-looking way.

Luckily, Margot or whatever her name is doesn't exist. She's just an amalgam of cosmetics ads, vague expectations, social media posts, and anxieties about failure.

Not actually existing is better for Sage. If she did exist in real life, she'd be secretly, desperately miserable. Living a life that is defined by some external standard of success that she doesn't share in her heart, she'd squander all her time and energy trying to live up to an ideal she can't remember subscribing to.

Plus, yuck, she'd be super annoying to hang out with.

Why are we trying to emulate someone we wouldn't even want to go to brunch with?

You *Already Know* How to Lean the Fuck Out

You know those guided meditation apps where they ask you to picture yourself in a peaceful forest? And you are supposed to Zen out—but all you can think about is how the cricket noises are jarringly loud and you have an itch on your elbow and is it a poison ivy rash or a mosquito bite or nothing and you're just attributing it to some mystery of nature because this soft-voiced lady keeps talking about the woods and you hate camping and did you remember to water the plants yesterday and do they need fertilizer soon?

We're going to do one of those guided meditations together, sort of.

I'd like you to think of a time when you gave yourself a break. When, by some miracle or twist of fate or decision of your own, there was a stint of time when no one was asking you to do shit for them. When you dropped some obligations. When you stopped, temporarily or permanently, trying so hard at something.

Maybe it happened in a planned way, like with a vacation. Maybe you did one of those all-inclusive thingies where you don't even have to think about the next activity or meal, you just drift along and someone supplies whatever you need. Or a week when your boss was out of town so you slacked off at work a bit, or a day when the rest of your family or all your roommates left to do some activity that you didn't do, so you found yourself alone with no company or duties.

Or maybe you were forced to stop. Maybe you were a committed athlete and you suffered an injury. Maybe you lost a job or got the flu. Or maybe a global pandemic shut the world down.

That last one, the global pandemic? That's the one that lifted things off my plate.

I teach at a college. For me, the first thing that happened was my spring break from school was extended an extra week. "Yes!" I thought. "Now I can do all the little tasks I'd meant to do during the first week of break but ran out of time!"

Please pity me, because I was excited to paint my cabinets and clean out my attic. Those aren't metaphors: Those are activities that actually used to get me excited.

But when the second week passed, and it became clear that COVID was a serious, deadly pandemic that was going to upend all our lives over the long term, my feelings changed.

Of course, the top layer of feelings was worry—about health and isolation and logistics and loved ones.

But underneath the worry level, some part of me felt free. At work, I was instructed to make my courses easier. Cut every reading and assignment that wasn't essential. Extend grace and leniency to my students. And above all, go easy on myself. "Lighten your demands on yourself," everyone was saying. "No one is expecting perfection right now."

In other words, lean the fuck out.

It didn't take more than a couple of days before I, and many others, started thinking, "Wait, shouldn't I always do this? Shouldn't I demand only what is essential from others, and never ask them to do extra just because I have the authority to do so? Shouldn't I extend grace and leniency to others, even when they're not suffering?"

Shouldn't I always go easy on myself? Is perfection ever necessary?

Another bit of grace that the universe was extending to everyone was that suddenly it was recognized that having children can be a challenge. Suddenly it was okay if your kids peeked into the background of your conference video call. Suddenly everyone noticed, dang, it's difficult to find childcare for your kids—a problem that, yes, was compounded by the pandemic but had always existed. Suddenly parents were permitted to say aloud, "I can't make it to that meeting because I don't have childcare at that time." Finally parents were admitting that they struggle to enforce screen limits or bedtimes or cleanup rules, and that their home lives are mostly chaotic.

Of course, a great deal of extra responsibility and stress was added to the lives of many, including frontline workers. And no one wants to go back to the bad old days of lockdown and extreme illness. But for those of us whose responsibilities decreased? It's okay to admit that that part felt great.

This book is about finding that little sliver of relief you felt—either when you were on vacation or when you made a decision to take a responsibility off your plate or even when you were experiencing some problem that limited your capacity to do shit. We're going to take that sliver of relief and expand it into a more fulfilling approach to life.

That's what it means to Lean the Fuck Out.

Let's keep the goals simple:

^

Do one thing
every day
~~that scares you.~~

MARY SCHMICH

Chapter 1

How History
Fucked Us Over

In a 2022 standup routine, the legendary comic Janeane Garofalo quipped, "When someone tells me I can't do something? [pause] I'm *grateful*."

Garofalo was channeling the slacker, Gen X vibe that predominated in the early '90s but was overtaken by the girlboss, go-get-'em, "just work harder" mainstream feminism we are more familiar with today.

But we have a lot to learn from our Lean Out forebears. They successfully resisted the ideas that work is good and that the more of it you do, the better.

The idea that if you're not working you're worthless is sort of fucking weird when you think about it. So how did we get here?

A Short-*ish* and Simple History of Why We Work *Too Hard*

Get out your notebooks, ladies. It's about to get a little historical in here. Lesson 1: The Bible.

Weirdly enough, although many of our other strict cultural norms originate there, you can't blame the Bible for our culture's devotion to hard labor. Because in the Bible, work is the enemy. Adam and Eve disobey God's command not to eat the fruit from a tree, and how does God punish them? With work! God says something like, "You guys, very uncool. Now you're not just going to have delicious fruit trees etc., but you're going to have to toil and sweat, and work is gonna suck." Even Jesus gets in on the work-hating. To paraphrase, he's like, "Yo, look at the fucking lilies in the field. Those guys don't do jack shit and look how awesome it works out for them. You people should be more like lilies. Stop working so much."

So, if even the Bible tells us we should hate work and advises us only to do it when it's strictly necessary, how did we get to where we are today, with the belief that work should be fulfilling and that having a strong work ethic is a good, virtuous trait? How did we get from God being like, "Brah, you gotta work now, fucking sucks, bro," to me, today, checking my work email while stopped at a red light during my commute home because I'm worried I won't respond to an after-work email quickly enough?

If you ask Max Weber, famed author of the 1904 long-ass sociology essay "The Protestant Ethic and the Spirit of Capitalism," it probably goes back a few hundred years to the dawn of modern capitalism. For Weber, it's all Martin Luther's fault (that is, the sixteenth-century Christian reformer Martin Luther, not to be confused with civil rights hero Martin Luther King Jr.).

Max Weber was a political economist—worth mentioning, a political economist who had experienced a very serious mental breakdown brought on by working too fucking hard—and he noticed that in traditional agricultural societies, even if you paid people extra, you couldn't get them to harvest more quickly or more efficiently. There was a certain amount that people were willing to work, enough to earn them a sufficient living, and beyond that, work ethic pretty much plateaued. More pay *did not work*. Farm workers were just like, "Overtime? Fuck you," or maybe, "No thanks," if they were feeling polite. If people's desire to work leveled out right when they received adequate pay, how did we get to the mega-billionaires with five mansions throughout the world still toiling on and on to get more?

For Weber, the introduction of the religious idea of predestination changed everything. Once people believed that there was no way to "good deed" your way into heaven, it started to feel like the holiest people were the ones who felt assured they *were* chosen for heaven. So ceaseless labor became a way to show how chosen you were—if you know you're getting into heaven, pushing a plow around all day doesn't seem so bad, so you're super cheerful about it.

The "best" people were the ones who didn't mind working, because they felt confident they would get their heavenly reward in the end.

The harder I work, the more ~~luck~~ *pit stains* I seem to have.

COLEMAN COX

Boom! Suddenly labor equals virtue. Fast-forward a few hundred years and I find myself excited when I have a day off work so I can clean my house—exchanging one form of labor for another, day in and day out.

The Protestant work ethic, or whatever we'd like to call its descendant—maybe the Post-Protestant Work-Is-Virtuous Vibe?—leads us to overwork, both at our paid jobs and at our unpaid domestic labor.

It also leads to funny social situations. The Post-Protestant Work-Is-Virtuous Vibe is why, if I bump into someone in the hallway at work and ask them how they are, they will always respond, "*Busy!*" Like yeah, we are all busy; this is not a lie. But the compulsion to frequently declare your own busyness is a by-product of a culture that says if you're super overworked, you're being a good person.

Of course, I'm paranoid my coworkers are just saying they're busy so they don't get stuck chatting with me. But that's an issue for my therapist, not for this book.

Feminism and the Pressure to *Lean In*

For women, it's not just the general "work is good" vibe pressuring us to lean in. Achieving the right to work outside the home has been a longtime goal of many feminists. Back in the eighteenth century, women (in particular, those who were not already forced to labor for others in servitude or service) politely cleared their throats and said something along the lines of, "Excuse me, but it would be super great if we could, you know, vote and go to school and own property and hold jobs other than seamstress. No worries if not! Thanks!" By the twentieth, when some of those rights had been secured, women raised their hands and were like, "Glad we can vote and whatnot, but when we said we wanted jobs, we didn't mean all the shittiest ones that men don't want to do. We want the good jobs, too. If it's not too much trouble. Sorry for being a nag, LOL."

Historically, it has really meant a lot to women to be able to work outside the home.

Today, the girlboss movement has promised women that if they work hard enough, they can make it to the tops of corporations and reach down to bring up all the rest of the women behind them. Aside from the problematic equivalency of happiness with money and power, and aside from the complete ignoring of the structural barriers that might prevent a woman from "making it" based on hard work, this idea further marries virtue with overwork. The idea that to help other women we must spend all our time and energy climbing a corporate ladder—or more aptly, a corporate escalator that sexism has stuck in the "down" mode—puts added pressure on women. It tricks us into thinking every extra hour logged at work is a donation to the feminist cause.

All the while, most women are still dealing with all the domestic crap they did before "defeat the corporate world" was added to the schedule. So after a regular day's work, and then the second shift of networking or moonlighting or pursuing a side hustle or taking on extra projects in order to be the best worker, many ladies are taking on a third shift of cooking, cleaning, childcare, and generally ensuring their households are top-notch as well.

Everyone agrees that this pressure is unsustainable over the long term. But too often the proposed solution is to find more and better ways to get things done. Productivity hacks.

Fuck productivity hacks.

Instead, we need to uncouple work from virtue. Each time we do our work fine, but not perfectly, letting our homes stay messy, leaving our t's uncrossed and our i's undotted, choosing leisure or joy over working ourselves to death, we need to claim that as a little moral (and even feminist) victory, rather than shaming ourselves as a failure.

When you have exhausted all possibilities, remember this: You haven't.

ROBERT SCHULLER

You're just exhausted.

Chapter 2

What's Wrong with Leaning In?

I would love nothing more than for women to be in charge of everything.

This is not really a criticism or rebuttal of *Lean In* or any other positive self-help book that has helped women do great things. It's also not a criticism or rebuttal of the author of that book—I'll leave that to everyone else. I mean, my heart weeps when I think about how fucking tired she must be at the end of each arduous day of leaning in. And I do a teensy bit hate her for making all my friends think that to get ahead, they must attend every meeting and make every decision and cut short maternity leave and stay on call all weekend and ignore their mental and physical health and hustle nonstop and girlboss girlboss girlboss.

The "lean in" solutions remind me of Louis Sachar's witty and weird children's novel, *Sideways Stories from the Wayside School* (1978). At Wayside, the meanest teacher keeps turning the students in her class into apples. Mrs. Gorf turns Joe into an apple for copying from John's paper, Todd into an apple for objecting to Joe's being turned into an apple, Terrence into an apple for falling out of his chair. She turns Eric into an apple for laughing and Stephen into an apple for crying.

I always get stuck thinking about a critical moment in the story: After Mrs. Gorf turns a bunch of students into literal freaking apples, what's the deal with the rest of the still-human kids? The Great Appling unfolds over days. It's surprising that no one does anything for so long.

My guess is, they were telling themselves that even though the apple-turning spree was unjust, at least it wasn't happening to them. And that even though they were stuck in an unjust system, they could, as individuals, figure a way out. I imagine myself sitting there as a little kid, surrounded by apples that used to be human children, thinking, "Mrs. Gorf is a little out of control here, but I'm a well-behaved girl. I'm sure I can figure out how to avoid being turned into an apple. These formerly children apples all did something wrong, however slight. *As long as I stay perfect*, Mrs. Gorf won't turn me into an apple."

We're all just sitting still, trying to be perfect, hoping the proverbial Mrs. Gorf doesn't turn us into metaphorical apples.

The Problem with Being a Try-Hard

This focus on individualism is the core (apple pun alert!) problem with the idea of leaning in.

Women who have ascended to power in our society have looked around and noticed: Hey, I'm sort of alone up here.

Women have been historically excluded from workplace leadership, along with the power and wealth that accompany it, and as a result, women still don't have wealth and power. At its base, the "lean in" ideology says, sure, there are all kinds of broad, systemic social problems that make workplaces exclusionary to women and advancement difficult or near impossible. We all agree on the problems. But the leaner-inners claim that the most effective solution is for women—individual women—to try really, really fucking hard. The leaner-inners believe that after all that trying hard, maybe those individual try-hards will get some power. The leaner-inners hope that then their power will just trickle down to other women through enlightened policies, like adding pregnancy parking spots to workplace parking lots.

There are quite a few problems with the "Try Hard to Get Ahead" approach.

Having individual women work three times as hard as they should need to, in the hopes of breaking through and pulling a few other women up behind them, is, first of all, unfair. Let's call out the complete double standard in the first place.

But second, it does nothing to address the system as a whole. It's the approach shared by the kids in Mrs. Gorf's class: Look around, say, "Ah yeah, this is pretty fucked up," and then hope you are personally exceptional enough to overcome it. Because it doesn't affect the underlying injustice, an individual's solution doesn't ultimately change much.

Women who have climbed to the tops of their fields often find it difficult to exert their energy bringing other women up behind them—because even at the top, the same pressures and sexism prevail.

The purpose of this book is to help us all become more aware of the times when we're being gaslit into thinking that we have the duty to lean in—to try harder in the face of difficulty or impossibility, to give it 110 percent, grit our teeth, and power our way through—when in reality, the best course of action is often to opt out.

But in general, yeah, women getting into power is a good idea.

This book is also not a criticism of ambition itself. You want to get out there and lean in to something? Then lean the fuck in, girl!

In fact, my staunch opinion is that the best thing women could do for each other is stop criticizing each other, and yes, I'm writing this sentence directly to Meghann on my local mommy Facebook group who often makes snide remarks about other people's parenting choices.

The problem is not leaning in itself. The problem is that we're leaning in every direction at once and being rewarded minimal or nonexistent returns for our efforts. Work demands compete with domestic duties, and in many cases we are shouldering an unfair balance of emotional labor both in the workplace and at home. And performing well at home or at work often leads to little growth or fulfillment—only more work, more performance expectations.

One of the big ideas of *Lean In* is that women should stop holding themselves back. The author challenges the reader to consider, *What could you do if you weren't so afraid?*

It's an intriguing question. I like it. But what if the problem wasn't that women were holding themselves back?

What if leaning in hasn't gotten us where we wanted to go because of broader structural problems?

Time to Unsubscribe

For the rest of this book, look for "Time to Unsubscribe" alerts. These little boxes will point out situations where you can feel totally fucking free to opt out of busting your ass to solve collective, social problems as an individual—and when you're being gaslit into thinking you need to take on the weight of the world.

Or, what if leaning in *did* get us somewhere, but once we arrived, we realized that version of success couldn't make us happy?

This book challenges the reader to consider a different question:

What could you do if you weren't so fucking exhausted?

Chapter 3

Aim <u>Lower</u> (at Home, at Work, *and* on Social Media)

We need to start by stating a fact that on one hand is obvious, but on the other, is very easy to lose sight of: You have value beyond your capacity to work.

Or, to put it a little more fun-ly: You're fucking awesome! You're rad! You're super cool, and if I knew you personally, I'd want to be your best friend!

You don't have to work yourself nonstop at home and at work and online to prove it!

The central tenet of the girlboss ethos can be summed up in three words: work work work. But it forgets that when we were encouraged to conquer the working world, nobody gave women a pass on domestic duties. Now here we are, still haunted by the ghosts of the old ideology that demands a perfect home while also laboring outside the home in a system that doesn't always reward us professionally for our efforts. We're still expected to keep a lovely, neat home; to have great taste and own nice stuff—and to make all the most sustainable choices so we can save the Earth to boot!

The message we've often internalized is, you have to be perfect at work and at home. And you must put that perfection on display (coyly! tastefully!) on social media.

But even girlbosses who want to take the world by storm need a break now and then. This chapter is about how to take a breath, notice when you're doing too much, and reclaim a life aside from all the work demands.

"Work"
Does Not Equal
"Worth"

The concept that nonstop work is virtuous permeates our culture and reaches most of us when we're pretty young. I remember a little song the summer camp counselors taught us when I was a kid. There are a million verses. It goes like this:

> Hi, my name is Jo, and I work in a button factory.
>
> One day, my boss came up to me and said, "Hi, Jo! Are you busy?" I said, "No."
>
> "Then turn the button with your left hand."

Okay, it's not a top ten hit, but we kids loved it. The boss keeps coming and asking if Jo is busy, and Jo keeps saying "no," and the boss keeps adding work. When you sing it, you do all the gestures of turning new buttons with new body parts that the boss keeps requesting. By the end of the song, you and Jo are turning buttons with your left hands, right hands, left feet, right feet, heads, butts, and noses. In the exciting conclusion, she finally admits to her boss that, yes, she is busy.

And Jo stops turning all those fucking buttons.

What is the point of this little ditty? Little kid me thought the educational purpose was to teach us the parts of the body, left from right, etc.

Adult me gets it: This is an analogy for the working world.

Why do we feel compelled to pretend we have an unlimited capacity for labor? It doesn't matter how many buttons we're already turning: We keep telling the boss that even though we are already turning buttons, we still have the bandwidth to add a little more work.

Possibly, this tendency to overwork ourselves comes from the fear of being fired. But take a look around your workplace. Has anyone been fired recently for, you know, not turning enough buttons at once? Although this varies a bit from industry to industry, for the most part it's considerably cheaper and easier to keep an underproductive employee than to recruit, hire, and train a new one—still risking that the new person will be no better.

There are a bunch of geniuses at your job who are working less hard than you for, the same pay. And if you're a woman, there are a bunch of dudes there working less for more pay.

I do know some people who've been fired from their jobs. Zero of them were fired because they weren't productive enough. They were all giving it 110 percent, very much sprinting in the rat race, but some financial reason caused the company to downsize. Their job security was entirely out of their control.

So we're probably working too hard, like poor Jo here, getting herself into the ludicrous situation of turning buttons with her butt, for some reason. Our culture has led us to equate working itself with virtue—selling us the idea that working hard is, in and of itself, good.

But who benefits from this culture of "giving it 110 percent"?

Spoiler alert: In most cases, not the worker!

I'm not cynical enough to start telling anyone, especially women, who have been historically excluded from well-compensated labor outside the home, to stop working hard at their jobs. (And if my boss is reading this book right now, rest assured: I work my little butt off! Also, boss, don't read the rest of this chapter.) I'd love nothing more than for the hardworking women of the world to get promoted en masse and take charge of all the companies and organizations.

But for all the talk of quiet quitting—that overblown phrase that essentially means having a job without letting it completely infiltrate and destroy your entire life—no one talks much about the quiet promoting that's been going on forever. If quiet quitting means trying to "get away with" doing a little less for the same pay, it pales in comparison to how the people in charge constantly, relentlessly try to "get away with" forcing workers to do more work without any more compensation.

You don't even need an exploitative workplace to feel work creeping into the nonwork part of your life. I really love my job and have very reasonable and considerate supervisors. But many evenings, after I've technically "clocked out," I find myself reading and responding to work emails. Or I'll sit down to enrich my life by reading a good book (that is a lie: I'll sit down to watch TV), and I'll think to myself, "I should probably read that report I didn't get to before I left work." And sometimes I'll even . . . read the report! Instead of enjoying my life!

In the era of the Great Resignation and quiet quitting, it can feel like the only respite from relentless work is to quit our jobs or totally slack off, stop caring, and idly wait to get fired for negligence.

To be honest, yeah, that would be the ultimate lean out. Just stop working altogether!

Unfortunately, this option works best only among the independently wealthy.

Signs You've Been Quiet Promoted

☆ You got more responsibilities at work, but no new job title and no increased pay. Congratulations on your quiet promotion!

☆ You got more responsibilities at work and a new job title but no increased pay. Congrats again!

☆ You got more responsibilities and increased pay at work, but the responsibilities increased twice as drastically as the pay. Wow! Kudos!

☆ You got more responsibilities and increased pay at work, but the responsibilities increased ten thousand times more drastically than the pay. What good fortune! You're killing it out there!

☆ Somebody quit or retired from your workplace, and instead of hiring a new person, they gave you the person's job functions without a new job title or increased pay. Woo-hoo! I'm so proud of you!

☆ Somebody at your job got promoted, and you started doing some or all of the work they used to do, but you weren't promoted into their old position. Another quiet promotion!!

Lies We Tell Ourselves	The Real Truth
I'm saving myself time tomorrow.	Ah, this is a beautiful temptation. Just respond to this email real quick tonight, then your workday will be easier tomorrow. But guess what: Everything you take off your plate today will be replaced with a new task tomorrow. There is no saving yourself "future time." The work is ceaseless.
I'll just do this real quick so I can stop worrying about it.	Hahaha, you're cute! You think there's an end to the work worry?! There's a whole army of worries lined up behind that one. And this army is only emboldened by your engagement with it. It retreats only when you ignore it.
Everyone is counting on me.	Reality check. Yes, this is a workplace, so someone may be counting on you for something. But is *everyone* counting on you for *everything*? Nope! Try not over-working yourself to death for a couple of days. You may be surprised to find the walls don't crumble. "Everyone" will be just fine.
My career depends on my ability to constantly work.	Rreenhh-rreenhh! (That's the sound of a game show "wrong answer" buzzer.) As a matter of fact, your career depends on your ability to stop working sometimes, claim some leisure and enjoyment for yourself, and avoid burnout.
But I love my job!	That's great! Me too! But life is long. We need to love other things too.

But you don't have to sacrifice an income, or even job satisfaction and commitment, to lean the fuck out of work. The first step is to silence the "button-turning song" in your head, that little voice that equates your self-worth with your willingness to work continuously, without rest, always being "on" and always saying "yes" to doing more.

In other words, mentally uncouple virtue and goodness from work. You're worthwhile no matter how hard you're able to work!

If you can't let go of work altogether, start with giving it 100 percent instead of 110 percent.

Time to Unsubscribe

Are you being overworked because your workplace is understaffed? That's some bullshit you can opt right the fuck out of. Not being able to do the work of seven people is not a personal failing! It's a structural economic problem that you can't solve by "giving it your all" and leaving yourself with nothing.

Turning **Off** *Work Brain*

Even once we've overcome the false equation of work with virtue, it can be hard work to stop working so hard.

A key to leaning the fuck out of work is giving yourself permission to let go at the end of a workday.

The problem is, we can't just snap our fingers and turn off work brain.

At the end of every workday,
we need to put on a mental suit of armor,
battle the work-worry monsters,
and rescue our brains from
the evil clutches of 24/7 work anxiety.

Admitting that work does not equal inherent goodness helps. Setting firm boundaries between work time and personal time helps. But it can also be helpful to develop a little "work is over" ritual.

A friend of mine always used to bike to and from work, but then his job converted to fully remote. He started having a lot of trouble ending his workday. Tasks kept coming in, so he kept completing tasks. And even after the work ended, he was still thinking about it.

So at 5 p.m. every day, he started taking a bike ride. In addition to restoring his pre-remote-work commute vibes, the physical activity slowed his work momentum and forced his brain to focus on something else.

I'm personally not ready to introduce that much exercise into my life—hopping on a bike every fucking day sounds worse to me than leaving work brain on indefinitely. But even a moderate physical shift can help you tap the work brakes. Here are some ideas:

☆ Make a to-do list of the things you need to do tomorrow. Sometimes making the worries concrete can relax you a bit. Or maybe the list will just freak you more. If that happens, burn the list.

☆ Use your commute home to call friends and family members and catch up on each other's lives. In a few short weeks, you can go from missing all your friends and feeling like you never have time for them to being intimately familiar with all their hot gossip.

☆ Turn on your favorite song. Blast it. Do a little "Work Is Over!" dance. *Dance like no one is watching. Honestly, what a weird thing to say; I hope no one is watching you.*

☆ Treat yourself to a special snack or drink. The after-work cocktail is a famous example, but a lovely fancy tea or coffee or seltzer could do the trick, too. In Argentina, after work everyone meets up with their friends in parks, and they chat while they sip yerba maté. I mean, yerba maté is disgusting, but it's otherwise a great idea.

☆ Remember Mister Rogers? He used to take off his blazer and put on a cozy sweater, then take off his work shoes and put on some comfy sneakers. But I get the feeling that his job was not very high stress. You may need to sit down and just change your shoes over and over again for about an hour.

☆ *Every day after work, build an effigy that symbolizes your job. Maybe a cloth stethoscope for doctors, a cardboard envelope for mail carriers, a wooden plow for farmers—you know, nothing too ambitious. Then burn it.* Yes, build and burn an effigy that symbolizes work every single day. Remember to keep a fire extinguisher on hand!

The point is, tell your body and mind: Body, mind, it's time to lean the fuck out of work for the day.

Clean Less

If you are naturally neat, congratulations! The world celebrates you.

Magazines with deceptive names like *Simple Clean* feature your perfect living room in their special Pretty Perfection issue.

Some people dream of success, while others wake up and work hard at it.

Still others dream of less success, a reliable dental plan, and a moment of fucking peace.

The Necessity of a Clothes Pile

Deep down, you know the truth: You and your clothes deserve to let loose. Traditional clothing storage is so confining. It's predicated on the extremely flawed premise that we only need two different kinds of storage. The typical bedroom assumes that you have some clothes you can fold and put into drawers, and some clothes that for one reason or another are not appropriate to fold and should therefore be hung in a closet.

This binary system is a completely inadequate approach to the way we actually live and the clothes we actually have. True, we all have some folded clothes and some hung-on-hangers clothes. But the binary clothing storage system overlooks each of the following storage needs:

☆ Clothes that are too bulky to fit in drawers but whose shoulders get weird creases in them when they're hung up.

☆ Clothes that you wore once or twice and maybe should wash, but there's a chance you'll want to wear them again before laundry day, so you don't want to put them in the hamper yet.

☆ Clothes that don't quite fit right now, but they might fit again within the next few years, so you should probably hang on to them.

★ Clothes you try on but then realize they have a stain on them, and you'll get around to trying to remove the stain at some point . . . but not today. And never today.

★ Clothes with a missing button or a mendable hole. *Someday you might wake up and be a completely different person, the type who replaces buttons and mends holes. Or maybe fairies will come and do it overnight.*

★ Clothes that you wear almost every day, so why bother putting them in the closet or in a drawer when you're just going to wear them again tomorrow?

★ Clothes that you're too tired to fold or put on a hanger. (So, basically all your clothes.)

★ Enter the domestic solution of your dreams: the clothes pile. I consider it the most important piece of bedroom furniture after the bed (which is the most important because . . . sleep, the ultimate lean the fuck out). The clothes pile just can't start on the floor, because then you have to bend over to pull stuff out of it.

★ I recommend a folding chair. It gives you the comforting illusion that your clothes pile is just a temporary fix, that someday all your clothes will be on hangers or neatly folded in a drawer.

★ Until then, they (like you) will be living their best life, luxuriating in a beautiful, messy heap with all their clothing friends.

But if you're like the rest of us, that shit is exhausting.

Before you give up your nights and weekends trying to whip your home into shape for the approval of all your neatest friends, just consider being fun and messy you.

You could (I'm lowering my voice) simply (I'm whispering this now) opt out of this cleaning compulsion altogether. My messiest friend lets the mess accumulate indefinitely. Going to her house is the *best*, because it's a true authentic mess that she never tries to conceal.

I might visit three other friends and say with wonder, "Wow, your place is so beautiful! You keep it so neat!" but my true admiration goes to my friend whose house feels genuinely comfortable and lived in—and who doesn't give a fuck what anyone thinks about it.

So really, the best way to lean the fuck out of cleaning is just not to clean. Ever. Just stop cleaning.

But I admit I'm not at that level of enlightenment yet. Sometimes I still want people to say with wonder, "Wow, your place is so beautiful! You keep it so neat!"

*Fooling everyone into thinking you're
neat and clean and have your life together
doesn't require you to ever actually clean.
You just need a place to dump all your junk quickly.*

My coffee table? It's an empty trunk. My end table? It's a smaller empty trunk. The walls of my dining room are lined with half-empty cabinets.

When I'm about to host a party or have parents or in-laws over for a visit, or when I've just grown tired of my own mess, it takes about five minutes to scoop all the mess up into my arms and dump it into the cabinets and trunks and closets. *Voilà!* A neat-as-fuck house.

Then, when the party's over, you can take everything out gradually, as needed. And anything that stays in the trunk or closet or cabinet more than a month or two, you probably don't need at all! Admit to yourself that you should just throw that shit out instead of constantly cleaning it up.

Keep *Less* Stuff

You own, undoubtedly, a few items that you have a great deal of affection for. A soft, well-worn bathrobe. A set of dishes handed down from the proverbial grandma. A little table lamp you found super cheap at a thrift store that's kinda weird and maybe objectively ugly but it's really "you" and wait, come to think of it, what does it say about you that you really vibe with a used $3 lime green lamp with a yellowing mismatched shade?

But aside from that handful of things that you really love, when you look around, you'll probably find a lot of your stuff just . . . accumulated. You don't remember where or how you got it, and you don't particularly like it, but it's there. You've likely faded into a functional, nearly invisible relationship with most of your stuff.

Might be time to break up with your shit.

I have loads of experience breaking up with stuff. For the first decade of my adult life, I lived in New York City. You've probably heard stories: The apartments are really fucking small. As you read this, unless you live in NYC, Boston, Washington DC, coastal California, or a few other random pockets of runaway real estate prices, you can probably purchase a very nice modest home with a monthly mortgage payment that's less than the monthly rate I paid for an eighty-square-foot studio in Manhattan with a shared bathroom in the hallway.

But I didn't mind. I learned two things from living in New York. First, obviously: I don't need much space. Nearly everyone probably needs less space than they think they do. And second: I don't need much stuff.

Lots of people dislike moving, but not me. Every time I've moved, I've received a rare gift: a completely different relationship with all my stuff. It's really easy to accumulate shit, even when you're broke, even when you live in a small space. (And it's way easier to accumulate shit when you have a lot of space. At the moment, I have an attic. It's a curse disguised as a blessing.)

Lean the Fuck Out Alternative Route: Embrace the Clutter

I've discussed leaning the fuck out of accumulating stuff, with a simple approach: Throw that shit out. But the opposite also works great for leaning the fuck out: Lean the fuck out of the bougie minimalist aesthetic that's been dominating the collective unconscious and making us feel sheepish about our affection for, you know, *stuff*. Do you like having lots of clutter? Embrace it! Flaunt it! Display your collection of elaborately painted mismatched vintage porcelain swan sculptures proudly! Lean the fuck out of the tired "less is more" décor mantra and prove to the world that *more* is actually more.

But when you move, you have to look at each and every thing in your life and say, "Am I seriously going to put this into a fucking box and literally carry it to a new neighborhood/borough/state and shove it into a drawer in my new home, then never look at it until the next time I'm moving and have to make this decision again?"

If you come visit me, you'll find a lot of throw pillows, books, and nearly dead houseplants, because those are the three objects I most love and can't bring myself to throw away. Otherwise, there's not a lot of shit. I'm ruthless about dumping my old stuff.

I subject every item in my house to what I call the Moving Test. Think of it as a slightly less adorable version of the life-changing magic of tidying up. The Moving Test is more like the Life-Changing Magic of Breaking Up with All the Stuff from Your Past That No Longer Has Anything to Do with Current You.

Saying Fuck You to Clutter

☆ What if you were moving? Would you want to carry this stupid little thing to your next home? If no, throw that shit away.

☆ Would you want to go to the trouble of finding a place for this thing to belong in a new gorgeous house? If no, throw that shit away.

✪ When you look at this thing, do you think, "I don't want to go to the trouble of throwing it out, but if throwing something out were less effort than keeping it, I would throw it out"? If yes, throw that shit away.

Incidentally, this test also works for romantic partners. Sure, he's right here at the moment, but if you were moving to Paris, would you want him to come with you?

But I'm warning you: Do NOT use the Moving Test as an excuse to throw away this book.

Post *and* Scroll Less

Walking through a city park one day, I noticed a group of young women having a picnic. They had nailed two stakes into the ground next to their blanket and hung a hand-lettered banner that read "Happy Birthday, Marta" between the stakes. They were all wearing white and yellow dresses and had flowers in their hair. The array of fruits and cheeses on their blanket was elegant and bright. I was so touched by the care they were taking for one another and for Marta—until I noticed they weren't talking. They weren't laughing. They weren't eating. They were positioning each other into flattering poses and snapping each other's pictures.

I know exactly how they feel. The other day I made a galette for dinner—butternut squash, sage, and caramelized onions mixed together and tucked inside a flaky buttery crust. Cooking fancy is rare for me, I put in a lot of fucking time, and this galette was divine. Yet I felt annoyed because I couldn't get the right lighting or angle for a good picture of its tantalizing beauty. What's even the point of cooking delicious food if you can't get a good photo of it?

I had to remind myself that I was going to, you know, *eat* the delicious food.

Why should you have to sell your fun experiences to anyone else?

Why should you have to convince some unholy mash-up of former coworkers, ex-boyfriends' aunts, cousins you haven't seen since you were five, total strangers, and actual friends—anyone, other than yourself—that you're living life right? You fucking know you are!

Imagine a world where you didn't know the selfie camera angle that most flattered your jawline. Where you could dig in to your restaurant meal the moment it's placed in front of you, rather than photographing it from twelve different angles first. Where you didn't have to package your children's gorgeousness into a photo shoot, or their tantrums into a relatable quip.

And most importantly, where you weren't able to quantify how much approval was being meted out, each moment, by each selfie and food pic and beautiful but amusingly flawed child.

Imagine the women I saw in the park were actually just celebrating their friend's birthday, not promoting their personal brands online.

Imagine just feeling good about something—without posting about it online to multiply the good feeling.

To get that feeling back, without denying ourselves the little dopamine hits we've become accustomed to getting from social media, we can lean out in small doses.

How to Lean the Fuck Out of Social Media

☆ Leave your phone at home one day. Ever do this by accident? After an initial panic, losing the weight of that cumbersome piece of metal feels like floating on air.

☆ Post an unflattering photo of yourself. You know the one I'm talking about. Put it out there.

☆ Time yourself. Scrolling, yes, can feel like it's sucking away your life force. But maybe you aren't wasting quite as much time staring at your little glowing rectangle as you think.

You can use an app tracker that will tell you how much time you spend on each app. (Yes, it's an app that tracks how much you use other apps. . . . Yes, I understand the irony of recommending an app to get you off apps. No, I'm not proud of myself.)

☆ Do other people's social media posts make you feel jealous? Here's a radical idea: That's fine. Stop trying to make yourself feel unambiguously happy about other people's successes.

Fighting envy on social media is a losing battle. Let yourself feel the feels. Say aloud, "I envy Lena's trip to Thailand."

Once you're no longer trying to suppress your negative reaction, you might be able to realize your envy is not too strong. The long flight, the digestive adjustments, the humidity and what it'll do to your hair? Do you really want to go to Thailand? Or, saying it aloud might make you realize, "Wow, I really want to go to Thailand." Knowing what you want is a good thing.

☆ Why waste your own time and energy trying to wean yourself off social media? Lean the fuck out of that— and have another app do it for you. You can use an app blocker to lock yourself out of whatever apps you hate but love but hate but love but hate but love using.

Fake it
'til you
~~make it.~~

MODERN PROVERB

*get tired of staying
up late applying
photo filters to
cover the under-eye
bags you got from
lack of sleep*

If We Talked to Each Other in Real Life the Way We Do on Social Media

Scenario A

Someone I Went to High School with but Never Talked to While We Were in High School: Happy birthday!!!

Me: Thank you! Sorry, what's your name? And wait, how did you get into my house?

Scenario B

Me: Honey, you are my rock, my best friend, the heart and soul that brings joy to my every day.

My Significant Other: Huh?

Me: I just wanted to let you, and also everyone, know that you are seriously, for real, the greatest thing that's ever happened to me.

SO: Oh my God, what's going on? Are you okay?

Me: Of course! I'm better than okay! Because you have supplied all the love and support that I could ever want or need.

SO: Wait, are you mad at me?

Me: Angry? With you? You've brought purpose and meaning to my life. You're my spark, my fun, the sweetest and most beautiful person I've ever met. I love you with all my heart and soul.

SO: Okay, I'm calling an ambulance right now. I think you're having a stroke.

Scenario C

Me: [wears an appealing outfit]

Some Man I Know: [winks, blows a kiss, holds up an eggplant]

Everyone: WTF, dude?

Me: [eyes turn into sideways v's facing each other; green stuff projects from my open mouth]

The point is, even if you're not ready to drop social media altogether, practice leaning out of the exhausting work of branding your life. You don't need to curate a shiny, filtered Insta-version of you.

Advance apologies for getting sentimental on you here, but this is the truth: The only "like" you need is your own.

Do Less

If you want to keep your fucking wits about you, free yourself from trying to solve everything and just embrace the stillness.

In the excellent classic film *Karate Kid Part II* (1986), Daniel accompanies his mentor Mr. Miyagi to the Japanese prefecture from which Miyagi hails, Okinawa. There they discover that Miyagi's erstwhile best friend Sato is still harboring a decades-old grudge against him and wants to have a karate fight to the death. As they leave their first threatening encounter with Sato, Daniel asks, "What are you gonna *do*? About Sato?"

"Nothing," replies the wise Mr. Miyagi.

A lot of times, the right solution to a problem is just, see if it goes the fuck away on its own.

Guess what, it worked great for Miyagi. Ordinarily, I wouldn't spoil the movie for you, but at this point you should have already run out and seen it based on my calling it an "excellent classic film" two paragraphs ago. Before Sato is able to make good on his promise to kill or be killed by Miyagi, a typhoon hits the island and Miyagi rescues Sato from being crushed under a, like, log or beam or something. And the air is cleared between them. Doing nothing? It worked perfectly.

Let's all channel our inner Miyagis.

Situations where doing nothing is a terrible idea:

☆ You smell smoke. Be sure to check if anything's on fire.

☆ (Related: You realize that something is on fire. Put it out.)

☆ You have a suspicious mole. Get that checked right away.

☆ Your Kohl's cash is expiring today. You gotta get out there and buy yourself a cheap-ass blouse, girl.

But other than these rare "do something immediately" situations, it's often best to channel your inner Miyagi and wait.

The seventeenth-century English poet John Milton wrote one of his most famous sonnets, "When I consider how my light is spent," when he was bummed out, understandably, about going blind in his forties. He imagines an encounter with God (a very big deal for a very religious seventeenth-century dude) where God is just like,

Chill, dude. I'm not even that impressed with everyone scurrying around trying to do every-fucking-thing.

The final line of the poem is God telling newly blind Milton, "They also serve who only stand and wait."

Here's to only standing and waiting.

I dwell in
stretchy leggings and a hoodie
~~Possibility.~~

EMILY DICKINSON

Chapter 4

The Joy of *not* Cooking

Cooking is a lot of work and it doesn't deserve you.
Spend the next twenty-four hours truly paying attention to how much time, energy, and thought you spend preparing and consuming food.

You wake up—boom! Hunger! Gotta find food right away. If there are other people in your house, a lot of times you have to feed them too. After you cook and eat breakfast, you have to put away the food and clean up the plates, wipe off the counter, and so on. Repeat for lunch. Repeat for dinner. Don't forget all the little hungers that crop up between meals. Life is short, and, by my very scientific estimate, we spend 85 to 90 percent of our time choosing, buying, cooking, eating, regretting, and cleaning up food.

Fuck. That.

I'm not going to pretend you can eliminate it completely. We all have to eat lots of times a day. That's not going to change. And it shouldn't! Eating is the fun part.

The problem is that some of us internalized the pressure to prepare something meticulous and intricate for every single one of those three to six eating sessions per day.

We've dropped the pointy bras and flare-skirt dresses and pumps, but we're still often holding ourselves up against an outdated model of the perfect domestic woman who supplies healthy, nutritious, interesting home-cooked meals with a sparkling smile *(ching!)* while also being expected to manage a career, coordinate the social calendars of everyone in the family *(and somehow magically locate every goddamn lost item in the entire house, on demand, the moment someone needs it).*

Even though we're keeping about a hundred plates spinning, we still often end up feeling guilty whenever we (inevitably) run out of time and fall short of the ideal—because it feels like we're shirking our "duties."

If we'd known we would be modern working women still dealing with old-fashioned housewife guilt, we could have insisted on at least keeping the social acceptance of day drinking. Instead, we're more likely screaming "FUCK!" at the kitchen counter because we splashed marinara sauce on our laptop.

Instead of aproning up, let's silence the little voice whispering that we should be cooking more or better.

Put away our cutting boards and wooden spoons.

Or better yet, burn the wooden utensils for fuel. Get a cozy little fire going and read a good book while you wait for delivery to arrive.

Time to drop your cookbooks and frying pans *(not literally, they'll hurt your feet)* and lean the fuck out of cooking. I'll show you how!

Lean *the Fuck* Out of Following Recipes

Recipes can kindly fuck off.

First, there's a giant list of ingredients. Someone, in other words, has the audacity to tell me what to buy at the grocery store. Frankly, it's rude, and we're already off on the wrong foot. But before you even go to the grocery store with your fancy recipe list, you have to look through your cabinets, fridge, freezer, and pantry to see what you already have so you don't buy more of the same.

I suspect that most of us have what I call "grocery store anxiety foods"—shelf-stable cabinet items that you often pass by in the grocery store, think to yourself "I wonder if I need [blank]," can't remember if you have any, then tell yourself, "What the hell, couldn't hurt to have an extra [blank]." That's how I ended up with a small drawer full of jars of capers, an ingredient I use maybe three times per annum; a whole corner of the cabinet stuffed with peanuts, making it appear as though I'm planning a vicious attack on my nut-allergic nephew; and three large tubes of wasabi, which is physically not a lot of wasabi but is a genuinely absurd amount for someone who does not ever, ever need wasabi. If you need a fuckload of wasabi, please come hang out at my house.

Sometimes a recipe will claim to have few ingredients, which is charming, but obviously bullshit. I am still going to have to purchase and assemble oats—old-fashioned, not quick!— wildflower honey, dark chocolate chips, and unsweetened coconut flakes, so let's not pretend they're doing me any favors. Recipes are also known to make big promises about how few pots or pans you'll use.

"One-pot chili" or "one-pan pasta"? Yeah, you are naming the absolute maximum number of pots and pans I was willing to use.

Congratulations.

A recipe attempts to act all nonchalant about its toniest ingredients.

"A few threads of saffron, if you have them." I know what you're not saying, babe, and it's that I'm an uncultured piece of garbage if I don't have a few threads of saffron.

Well, joke's on you. I don't even know what a thread of saffron is.

Cooking is like love. It should be entered into with abandon or not at all.

HARRIET VAN HORNE
(1956, *Vogue* magazine, "Not for Jiffy Cooks")

So...not at all then.

One more major problem with the ingredient lists of recipes: A lot of times they sneak instructions into the recipe list, when clearly the ingredient itself requires a very distinct separate culinary step. For example, "two onions, minced." Are you fucking kidding me? And then when you get to the onion part of the instructions, it's just assumed you have already minced the onions? What do you think my life is like, recipe? I don't have a sous chef by my side every time I enter the kitchen.

In any event, imagine you're a patient, rich superhero and you have managed to procure and assemble all the ingredients, diced them into whatever shapes and sizes the tyranny of the ingredient list has demanded. I applaud you; you are a legend.

But you're not done yet.

After the ingredient list, recipes fall into two categories:

#1 dirty lying recipes that severely underestimate how long it will take to actually get food on the table

#2 mind-fuck recipes that deceive you with artfully hidden cook times. They just wait for you to start a recipe while nearly blind and starving, only to find out halfway through that it requires 90 minutes of oven roasting.

Both approaches to recipe timing are terrible, of course. And neither approach solves the problem of recipe timing, which is that recipes take time to follow. And I don't want to spend any fucking time cooking.

The worst part about recipe instructions is that they won't do you the courtesy of reminding you how much of each ingredient they had told you to use. The instructions will be like "sauté the garlic" rather than "sauté the aforementioned two cloves of minced garlic." So each and every time you do a new step, you have to re-find the ingredients mentioned in the accursed ingredient list.

The ingredient list is not arranged in a helpful way, so you just have to scan it over and over like a caged hamster on a wheel.

Except it's worse, because when the hamster gets tired he can stop and take a little nap, but you're stuck cooking. Sometimes the ingredient list is placed (infuriatingly) on the page before the recipe directions. Sometimes your kid is helping you, and in a desperate attempt to get help, you say, "How much garlic was I supposed to put in?" And your kid says some kid version of "How the fuck should I know?" which is not helpful, but fair.

Once you've completed this torture, I hardly need to mention that what you come out with looks nothing like the fucking picture.

Cooking with kids is not just about ingredients, recipes, and cooking. It's about harnessing imagination, empowerment, the self-control to stop yourself from ^ **and creativity.** screaming in rage when your kid dumps a pound of flour on the floor,

GUY FIERI

Get Other People in Your House to Do Some of the _Fucking_ Cooking

One of the most effective ways to avoid cooking is to have other people cook instead.

The trouble is, everybody hates cooking. Or, to be more accurate, given the choice between cooking and doing whatever the fuck they want, everyone would rather be doing whatever the fuck they want while someone else cooks.

Ways to coerce the people you live with to cook for you:

 # 1 Asking nicely always seems like a good first step. I mean, it never fucking works, but it's a sweet idea.

#2 And you know what? You shouldn't even have to ask. If you shoulder too much of the cooking burden in a multi-person house, I'm angry on your behalf about whatever shit went down that caused this imbalance. Don't even ask nicely. Just proceed to the more manipulative suggestions below.

#3 If you have kids in the house, tell them they can only use their screens on the nights they cook the family dinner. Your kids will cook you dinner, then they'll leave you alone the rest of the night. Double lean out!

#4 Get really, really terrible at cooking.

Self-sabotage every meal.

Put in sugar instead of salt, and vice versa. Let the cream curdle a bit. Boil pasta for double what the box says, then add five more minutes. Then the next time you cook, boil pasta for half the time the box says. If it gets this far, the next time, don't even boil it at all. Just mix uncooked noodles with cold canned sauce.

#5 Lysistrata anyone in the household you're sleeping with. In the ancient Greek play *Lysistrata* by Aristophanes, the women were sick and tired of the Peloponnesian War. Badass Athenian Lysistrata called a big meeting of all Greek women, and they resolved to withhold sex until the war ended. This is hardly even a spoiler: It worked great. The war ended.

If you take the Lysistrata approach to demanding cooking, be sure to withhold sex until your partner actually gets good at cooking.

Don't give in at microwaved hot dogs. You need a reasonably well-executed risotto.

And is it a double standard that you will not be reciprocating with a risotto of your own? Damn right it is. Enjoy that double-standard risotto and the consequent sex.

Pay Less, Cook Less

Unfortunately, I'm not here announcing that Payless ShoeSource has converted all its failing shoe stores into food stores. Imagine what a Payless FoodSource would look like: rows and rows of cheap food made from very questionable ingredients, some in containers but some just sitting out on the shelf, and somewhere buried in the steaming piles of poorly organized semi-edible food would sometimes be an amazing find that would always convince you it was worth it to come back again next time.

By "pay less," I'm talking about restaurants and takeout.

The easiest way to cook less is to have other people cook for you more.

Takeout is by far the biggest shortcut to leaning the fuck out of cooking.

But realistically, how often can/should an ordinary girl like me or you order takeout? I'm not an economist, but I know that it's not super cost-effective to order takeout every night. Nor am I a doctor, but I know eating takeout every night is not super-duper conducive to being in good health.

I have the perfect solution to solve both the economic and the medical problems: Get takeout and/or go to restaurants on random Monday, Tuesday, and Wednesday nights.

I feel sorry for Monday, Tuesday, and Wednesday nights. I want them to have a seat at the table when it comes to takeout.

My sympathy has nothing to do with me never having a cafeteria table to sit at in high school.

Every restaurant in my town has some kind of ridiculous food special on at least one of these nights. Half-price burgers if you buy a beer? You betcha. Any appetizer for $5? Sweetie, did you know you can just eat appetizers for your meal? It's the loophole the restaurant fat cats don't want you to know about.

I'm partial to my local Mexican restaurant's Taco Tuesday. The tacos are $1 each on Tuesdays. (Okay, at press time, the price had just increased to $1.50 per taco due to inflation, but still. It's important to accumulate a certain amount of things you can say "in my day, _____ cost _____ " about. So for me, it's "In my day, tacos cost $1!"

My point is: Go to Taco Tuesday. You'll be stuffed for $3 to $4.

And you won't have cooked a goddamn thing.

Fuck It ~~or~~ Fake It?

No matter how good she gets at leaning the fuck out, there comes a time in every busy person's life when cooking seems unavoidable. Potluck dinners. Hosting parties. There's always a backyard barbecue where they say "Don't bring anything, just yourselves!" but you bring yourself, everyone else brings an elaborate homemade casserole, wholesome salad, or award-worthy dessert, and you feel like an asshole.

The pinnacle of leaning the fuck out in these situations is just saying "fuck it" and not cooking anyway.

Potluck dinner? Stop at the grocery store on the way there. Grocery stores sell prepared food that's 1,000 percent better than anything I'm willing to bother making.

Hosting a party? Fun! Good for you! Get it catered. By which I mean, order a couple pizzas. And serve it on paper plates. Do you have any idea how delicious pizza is?

Backyard barbecue? They SAID to just bring yourself. Wouldn't society operate so much better if we all said what we meant and responded to the honest words that others said instead of what we guess is going on between the lines? In fact, by not bringing food, you're actually performing a service to humanity. You'll lean the fuck out and potentially be named humanitarian of the year!

And if you find yourself in the very rare situation where you can't say fuck it, time to fake it. Spoon that grocery store potato salad into your own fancy bowl on your way to the potluck or barbecue.

And remember the charcuterie trick. Serve bread, cheese, and fucking olives for a meal, and if you call it "charcuterie," it's legit.

Dump a couple Lunchables onto a fancy plate? Yup, that's charcuterie. Go for it.

What If You Like Cooking?

It's a rotten, painful truth, but I should probably acknowledge that some people actually like cooking.

You may like cooking if you:

a.) felt genuine concern for me, earlier in the chapter, when I said I don't have any saffron threads in my cupboard.

b.) wanted to leap to the defense of the evil recipe writers, because you actually love how recipes are laid out and you don't think recipe writers are cruel sadists out to ruin would-be chefs' evenings.

c.) thought to yourself, "Why would anyone pay $1 for a taco on Taco Tuesday when one can simply procure the twelve ingredients necessary to make a variety of kinds of tacos and spend forty-five minutes cooking and assembling them oneself?"

If you answered a, b, or c, you probably still don't truly like cooking—it's very rare. But if you are a, b, and c … yes, you might just like to fucking cook??

I confess I have sometimes imagined that I like cooking.

However, in reality, two things are true:

#1 I like eating.

#2 I like praise.

So, I want to eat delicious things all the time, and I want people to tell me I did something really well, like cooking a meal or dessert.

That ain't the same as liking to cook.

If you feel like maybe you enjoy cooking, I have some bad news for you: You might not actually like cooking. You can give yourself a test: Ask yourself, if no one was around, no one could see what you were doing, money was no concern, and health was no concern, what would you do for dinner?

To be clear, you are NOT allowed to post a picture of your meal to social media. This is a secret, no-budget-limit, magically no health effects meal.

What I would do if my self-worth wasn't tied up in cooking:

 # 1 If there were a way to sort of upload my history of food preferences into a computer and then have an algorithm tell me what food to choose for dinner each night, I would do it in a second. The emotional labor of choosing meals is far too much.

#2 Once the algorithm is properly functioning, I'd hire a world-renowned chef to privately cook me the dinner of my choice.

#3 (If the algorithm is not functioning for any reason— namely because it had not been invented, I'd still just tell the chef to surprise me so I wouldn't have to bother choosing the meal. In case I'm not being clear: Choosing what's for dinner fucking sucks.)

#4 If no chefs were available, I'd order takeout. I'd tell myself I'm trying something new, but each time I'd order a reliable favorite—in my case, anything on the menu with broccoli rabe, or gnocchi, or Thai basil, or chorizo, or a chocolate and peanut butter combination.

#5 If no private chefs and no restaurants were available, I'd just microwave myself a hot dog or a frozen burrito or something.

There is no scenario in which I'd cook an elaborate meal for me and only me. I'd say it would probably take me about a month on the private chef/takeout/microwave burrito plan before it occurred to me that it might be fun, for a change, to cook for myself.

In other words, I'll tell you what I would not do:

COOK.

So double-check with yourself: Do you actually like to cook, or do you just like to eat and receive praise?

If after all this, you're still convinced you like to cook, can you lean in to cooking?

Abso-fucking-lutely, babe! This book is all about no longer doing the shit you hate to make time for the stuff you actually like to do. So go ahead, cook your little heart out!

**A dream
does not
become reality
through magic;
it takes sweat,
determination,
and hard work.**
^
*and a willingness to
fail epically in most
other areas of life*

Don't Clean Up
After You Cook

There are very strict rules about who washes the dishes and cleans up the kitchen, but they're not what you think they are. In the great debate about who should wash the dishes, everyone has a very strong opinion, and that opinion is always, "Someone other than me should wash the dishes."

I'm here to settle the matter once and for all.

The humor writer Robert Benchley said, "There are two kinds of people in the world: those who divide the world into two kinds of people, and those who don't." I'm the former, here to tell you that there are two kinds of households: the ones who have achieved some kind of equity regarding who has to do the shitty, time-consuming labor of cooking the meals, and those who have one person do it almost every night.

To figure out who, according to universal laws of justice, has to wash the dishes, you need to first identify which kind of household you are. If one person does most of the cooking, that person never, and I mean never, has to wash the dishes for the meal they cooked. In primary cook situations, the main household cook gets to leave whatever disaster of soiled pots and pans and opened eggshells and tomato stems has occurred.

Because damn, they (often she) just cooked everyone dinner! She fucking earned a sit-down.

So the first part of the cleanup rule is maybe what you already thought it was:

The cook should never have to clean the kitchen.

But the "the cook never cleans up the kitchen" rule has one very firm exception. If everyone in your home cooks about equally, it is imperative that the cook be responsible for washing the dishes and cleaning up their own kitchen mess. And I'm sure you know why. When everyone carries their cooking load but doesn't have to clean up after themselves, you know there's going to be one asshole who absolutely maximizes the number of pots and pans and spatulas and cutting boards. The cooking asshole will take out the lemon squeezer to squeeze a lemon—fine. Maybe extraneous, but not a violation. But then the cooking asshole will take out the lime squeezer while prepping the same meal to squeeze a lime—it's the same thing but just green!

It's the cooking asshole who always burns the rice into the bottom of the pot and doesn't bother soaking it.

My point is, in cooking-equality households, it's completely unfair for someone else in the household to get stuck unsticking that pot.

So, the rule, in sum, is: Households with good cooking duty equality, wash the dishes the night you cook; households who lean too heavily on one cook, someone besides the cook washes dishes. You're welcome!

Becoming a *Badass* Batch Bitch

There's a slight chance you might run out of money to buy takeout, or you don't have anyone else in your house to cook for you, or you actually just want homemade food every now and again. This is sad, because cooking sucks and the thing that's the worst about it is that you have to do it so many times a day, every goddamn day.

A lot of people get around this bullshit by doing all (or most) of their cooking at once. For example, some people cook all their dinners for the week on a Sunday night.

This makes good sense, both philosophically and economically. The eighteenth-century Scottish philosopher Adam Smith (Yeah, you heard me. We're talking about eighteenth-century Scottish philosophers right now) popularized the concept of division of labor: the idea that goods are produced more efficiently if different people perform the discrete tasks, rather than having one person do every fucking thing.

So, imagine you want, I don't know, a table. You could have one fucking dude—or, more likely, a woman—drive out to the forest, cut down a tree, shave off the leaves and bark or whatever, haul it into a truck, drive it to your house, whittle all the branches down into leg shapes and the tabletop shape, mine some kind of metal from, uh, mountains or wherever metal comes from, forge the metal into nails, hammer nails into the legs to stick them onto the tabletop, sand it all down, and *voilà*! It's been seventy-eight years but a table has been made.

No, of course you'd have different people who were experts at each task do those tasks. That means one person is just hammering table legs onto tabletops, all day long, day in and day out, but it means a shit-ton of tables are made during the time it would have taken one person to make one table.

The same holds true for how you structure your week.

> *It doesn't make sense to call it division of labor anymore, unless you have multiple personalities.*

(If you do have multiple personalities, just off-load annoying tasks like cooking to the biggest bitch out of all your personalities.) When it's just you getting shit done, division of labor is called "batching."

My point is, if you put together a bunch of dinners over like three hours on a Sunday night, you don't have to deal with that shit for the rest of the week. Big mushy meals that can be in a big ziplock bag all week and the slow cooker all day work best for batching. But also you can do food batching that's just like chopping all the fucking onions you'll need that week. That way you're only crying over onions once a week, leaving all the other days for you to cry about non-onion-related woes.

The Economy of Scale, *Motherfucker*

Let's imagine you lose your mind some night and decide to cook an elaborate meal. You may even follow a godforsaken recipe, despite my litany of complaints about them above. Here's how to bank that temporary leaning in so you can lean the fuck out later: Leverage the economy of scale. The economy of scale is, unsurprisingly, an economics term that means, basically, a business can save on costs (and therefore increase profits) by increasing how much it produces. In other words, once you're going to all the fucking trouble of building and selling 100 tables, it may ultimately be more profitable to build and sell like 1,000 tables.

The same holds true for your bright idea to cook a big-deal meal. You're reading the recipe and buying all the goddamn ingredients they're insisting on, you've got the cutting board and knife and pots and pans and stuff out, somebody's going to have to clean up all this shit (to review: you if cooking is equitable in your house, someone else if it's not)—you've made a pretty big initial investment in supplies and time.

I implore you, don't just cook it for one or two or three or four or however many mouths you have to feed.

Double. That. Recipe. Or really, triple or quadruple it. Then you're operating within the economy of scale: You're getting a return of two or three or four meals for the investment of one cooking session. Stow the leftovers in your fridge and you can return to them in a couple days for a fancy, or at least fancy-ish, nostalgia meal. (Yes, I am trying to rebrand leftovers as "nostalgia meals.") Also, don't forget about your buddy the freezer.

Hint: Sometimes it helps to put the extra second meal into fridge storage before you start eating the first edition. Because the big risk with this plan is that if you do a really good job with the food, you could end up just eating a double portion.

Go Easy on Yourself.

Everyone leans in on cooking by accident every now and then. Just the other night, it was my turn to cook dinner. I decided to make something super easy that involved mostly microwaving stuff and very little cleanup. But then, being an idiot, I took out my phone and started scrolling. Wouldn't you know, almost immediately I saw a recipe for corn fritters that looked delicious. Before I knew it, I was grating cheese, chopping fresh herbs, and pulling literal fucking flour out of my cabinet.

The review the corn fritters got from my picky eater kid? "These are okay but I wish we could just have baby carrots instead."

My point is, nobody's perfect. As hard as we try not to try, sometimes we find ourselves trying much harder than we need to without even realizing it, as if in a trance. It's important to forgive yourself for those times when you do go above and beyond.

You can always lean the fuck out next time.

The most essential part of my day is a ~~proper~~ dinner.
I didn't waste my valuable time ^cooking

RACHAEL RAY

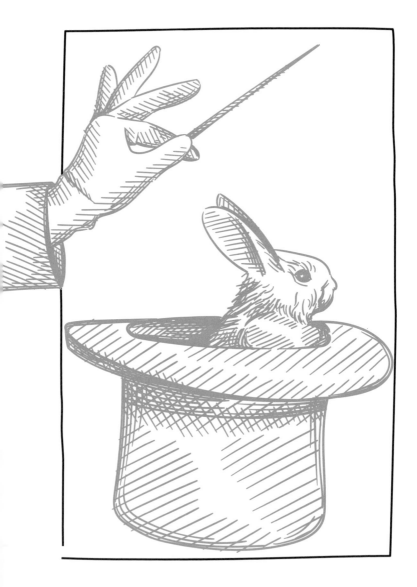

Chapter 5

The Magic
of *Do-Less*
Parenting

Welcome to the age of high parenting expectations, low parenting resources.

As far as I can remember from my childhood, parenting used to consist of arranging transportation to and from school and more or less keeping the child alive. During summers, I was let out of the house in the morning and called back, by a literal yelling of my name out the back door, when dinner was ready. (My parents could not be reached for comment. Details about the historical ease of parenting remain unverified.)

Today we're expected to know everything about our kids by monitoring the bejesus out of them at all times. From the second they're born, the attachment parenting and breast-is-best crowds insist that the best way to parent is to affix the child to your body—and once the kids get older, it's not much different. Our dear offspring supposedly need constant supervision, entertainment, dispute arbitration, and intellectual enrichment. When they're old enough to leave the house without you, they apparently need a smartphone that tracks their location. I have seen actual parenting advice, many times repeated, that the best way to let your kids enjoy screen time is to watch their shows and movies along with them, so you can talk with them about the content afterward.

As if the very reason I'm putting them in front of a screen is not to get away from those adored but exhausting little creatures for a few fleeting moments.

Meanwhile, as careers and cultural shifts have driven us further away from our extended families, the days of just dropping them off with a grandparent or plopping them down with a gaggle of cousins are gone.

Unless you have a live-in nanny and two six-figure incomes, dependable and affordable childcare remains a fantasy—like my recurring belief that bangs look good on me, tragically shattered every time I cut myself bangs.

Of course, it's not easy to just, you know, stop parenting. You can give up cooking fancy dinners or cleaning your house or working overtime, but having kids is a different order of magnitude—there's an actual real-life human at stake.

So how can we lean the fuck out of this modern era of overly attached, Velcro-style, helicopter parenting?

A Novel Idea: Just *Don't* Have Kids

When a lot of my friends were pregnant, they got really tired of being pregnant. "Get this thing outta me!" was a common refrain.

I think this sentiment had something to do with the fact that being pregnant is incredibly uncomfortable. When I say "uncomfortable," I don't mean it in the sense of "not comfortable." I'm using "uncomfortable" the way gynecologists use it when they're warning you they're about to stab your cervix with whatever torture device they use for Pap smears. "This might be a little 'uncomfortable,'" they say, meaning it's going to hurt like hell.

Pregnancy, you'd think, would mostly include whatever pain accompanies carrying a fifteen-pound bowling ball around all day: back pain, hip pain, belly-stretching pain, the esophageal hellfire of Tums-resistant heartburn. It does cause that.

If only that were all the pain.

Wait until you see your feet. Mine looked like two loaves of bread, browned and spilling out of the loaf pan. I felt like they would explode. In fact, I asked the doctor if it was possible my feet would explode. She said no, but advised me that I might want to avoid salt for a while. "SALT IS ALL I HAVE RIGHT NOW!" I screamed.

In short, being pregnant is what we euphemistically call "uncomfortable."

However, while my pregnant friends said, "Get this thing outta me," I took a very different approach. I foresaw—very correctly and brilliantly, if I do say so—that the discomforts attendant with pregnancy would be nothing compared with the intrusions of having a full-on human to take care of for a minimum of eighteen years. I prayed to every god available, none of whom I believe in, that I would simply stay pregnant forever.

Here's the hard truth: Having kids gobbles up 99.5 percent of what I used to consider my free time.

All of this is to say the most foolproof method of parenting less is, don't have kids. Yes, it's too late for many of us. (And as much as I begrudge admitting it, most of us who have kids don't regret it, and not only because of the cultural pressure to say you love having kids—most of us really do.) I will have plenty of advice and thoughts in this chapter for anyone already "fortunate" enough to have littles or already committed to procuring one or seven eventually.

But the truth is, choosing to go childless is one of the most effective ways to lean the fuck out.

Every study that's ever been done on happiness has concluded that people who don't have children are happier throughout the course of their lives. Does that sound weird? Look it up. I'm not citing any particular studies because every longitudinal study of human happiness conclusively confirms it: Childlessness improves well-being.

Leave Your Kids *the Fuck* Alone

My son was sitting on the dining room table, his butt parked right next to an open cellophane bag of LEGOs. According to physics' lesser-known fourth law of motion, a bag of LEGOs that is at rest at the edge of a table will be put into motion by the equal and opposite action of a nearby child.

Being a clever, cautious mom, I decided to preempt the coming disaster. I leaned across the table to move the LEGOs out of reach of my son's unwieldy limbs.

And of course I knocked over the entire bag myself.

This is Lean the Fuck Out 101. I could have just left both the LEGOs and my kid alone. The worst thing that was going to happen was that my kid would knock over the LEGOs. Then he would have had to pick them up instead of me, which would have been a fantastic outcome.

The truth is, had I not done or said anything, likely nothing at all would have happened. No LEGOs on the floor, no lessons learned, just a kid, sitting on the table with zero consequences, and a mom, controlling a little less, disseminating fewer worries, clearing some productive space in her mind and her kid's.

A kid sitting on a table, a mom leaning the fuck out.

The LEGO story is just one example of how we could be parenting a whole lot less than we are.

Here's a simple five-point checklist for determining whether to intervene in children's choices:

☆ Is the child on fire?

☆ Is the child playing with matches?

☆ Is the child holding a weapon?

☆ Is the child playing in traffic?

☆ Is the child on fire standing in traffic holding a weapon in one hand and matches in the other?

If the answer to all these questions is "no," I'd let them carry on as they are.

In fact, I could be convinced to remove the "playing with matches" criterion. It's actually kind of hard to light a match. I bet my kids probably couldn't even start a fire if they got their hands on a matchbook.

8 Things to Do Right This Second
⋮ Instead of Having Kids ⋮

~~~~~~~~~

#1 Get a dog (Shorter commitment, slightly less needy, less smelly than diapered and teenaged versions of human offspring.)

#2 Get a cat (A species confident it's better than people and willing to let you know.)

#3 Go get a massage (Now, and whenever you want, because you have enough time and money if you do it instead of having kids.)

#4 Go on a date (Please, for me, go to a place kids hate. Fancy prix fixe dinners in tiny quiet restaurants. Movies with no animation or explosions or people randomly bursting into stupid songs. A museum where they're having a little event and you get to have a cocktail in the lobby. I swear these things used to be part of my life.)

#5 Sign up for a class at a local arts center or community college (Instead of carting your kid around to practices and rehearsals and playdates with friends—friends, like what I used to have—you can actually think about what you might like to do with your time, and then just, like, do it.)

#6 Get a houseplant (Still provides companionship, and the engrossing challenge of keeping something alive, with considerably lower stakes.)

#7 Go on a faraway vacation (Did you know that for every kid you have, you have to buy an additional plane ticket? So if you have one kid, you have to buy a ticket for yourself and the kid. And if you have two, you have to buy three tickets. And if you have three kids . . . Oh who are we kidding, you're never flying somewhere again.)

#8 Keep doing whatever the fuck you want to do, day in and day out, for the <u>rest of your life</u>

What Can I *Dooooooooo*?

Every kid I know has their own unique whine of boredom. Sometimes it's "There's nothing to doooo!" or "I'm bo-ored." My kids say, "What can I do?" and hold out the "do" for the exact amount of seconds required to drive me out of my fucking mind.

Occasionally I'll execute some amazing, heroic parenting move, like a craft project or reading an actual book to my kids. And then immediately upon us finishing the should-be-award-winning mom-led activity, one of my kids will launch directly into "What can I dooooo?"

The problem with most modern-day spawn is not that they get bored. We get it—everybody gets bored. And they haven't been alive too long; they sort of suck at everything, including entertaining themselves.

The problem is their unshakable conviction that my job as their parent is to entertain them at all times.

Not only am I expected to feed them, love them, dress them, bathe them, bring them to school and enriching activities, and protect them from injury and death, but apparently I also must keep a spontaneous vaudeville act going at all times.

"Are you not entertained?" I scream, equally as exhausted as Russell Crowe in *Gladiator* right after he fights off all the competitors in the arena. "Are you not entertained? Is this not why you are here?"

It may be why they're here (to be entertained), but it's definitely not why we're here (to entertain them on demand).

You have value beyond your capacity to entertain your children. You're allowed to enjoy your life, or even less ambitiously, just pay your bills in silence now and again!

It's high time we stopped feeling guilty every time we choose something else over doing backflips to make our kids stop whining.

You are probably not going to believe the following anecdote is true, but I swear on all that is holy, namely Fräulein Maria in *The Sound of Music*, that it is. My kids were hissing some "what can I dooooooo's" at me, and I just calmly said, "I will not be providing you with something to do. You have to figure out what to do yourself."

"But there's nothing to dooooo. I'm bo-ored," they of course replied.

"I will not be providing you with something to do. You have to figure out what to do yourself," I repeated. "And if you ask me what to do one more time, no dessert."

Leaning Even Further Out: Stop Buying LEGOs!

Why are LEGOs even a thing?

When someone gives my kids one of these parent-torture boxes, I internally groan as I nudge my kid and hiss, "Remember to say thank you!" You open up a box of LEGOs and find 7,000 tiny plastic pieces that mostly look the same but have tiny variations that will become crucial during assembly—a very mean reminder that you need reading glasses. If you drop one of the 7,000 pieces on the floor, it will, by magic or physics, roll under the radiator and never be seen again. If you have a cat, and I have two, the cat will bat these things across the room, paw them into their mouths, and chew them up. I don't even know what dogs do to LEGOs, but I assume it's a slightly stinkier and slobbery-er version of what cats do.

In the very unlikely event that you are able to keep all 7,000 pieces in your possession, next you'll be treated to a 573-page booklet that supposedly explains how to assemble these little plastic nightmares into a bigger, supposedly fun toy. But the booklet will not have any words, just extremely confusing and ambiguous illustrations.

Neither you nor your child will understand these illustrations.

In classic lean the fuck out style, you might encourage your kid to complete this task on their own. That way, you will have a little time to yourself to pursue your own hobbies—not just the parenting "hobbies" of cleaning up your kid's other toys or assembling IKEA furniture, the grown-up version of "playing" with LEGOs—but honest-to-goodness fulfilling leisure activities like pottery and hiking and learning a new language. Your kid, especially if they've become accustomed to your leaning the fuck out of parenting, will be more than happy to put together the LEGOs on their own.

But this can lead to new problems within minutes.

You may hear, "Mommy, can you help me find this piece?" To which you can answer, "Fuck no, kid! I can barely see those microscopic things."

You may hear, "Mommy, I messed up! Can you pull these two pieces apart?" To which you can answer, "Fuck no, kid! Those two microscopic pieces of plastic are stuck together tighter than the sperm and egg that created you. To separate them, we'll need, what? Dental floss? A laser? Forget it."

Or you may hear, "Mommy, I can't do it! I'm stupid!" To which you should answer, "Aw, sweetie, you're not stupid!"

But you are permitted to think, "Wait . . . is my child stupid?"

After hours of struggle, you and/or the child will finally succeed in correctly assembling a toy from the 7,000 tiny pieces and the 573 pages of directions. And for one fleeting moment, you'll think, "Wow. This is actually kind of cool."

Last, your kid will play with their assembled LEGO thing for four seconds, then drop it. It will fragment back into its 7,000 component parts. Your child will cry.

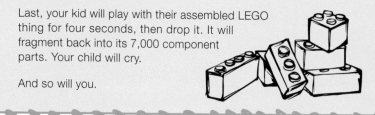

And so will you.

The threat of withholding sugar is pretty much my only parenting technique. Yes, I know you're not supposed to threaten children, and I know you're not supposed to leverage unhealthy food as either reward or punishment.

But, listen, this mom is pretty fucking tired and gave up on the complicated reward charts and sophisticated parenting techniques the second she realized the formula "If you [blank], no dessert" works every time.

Or at least, it worked this time. They left me alone.

This next part is what seems unbelievable. After they slunk away, dejected that their vile mother would not be performing a trapeze act for their entertainment, they found the most adorable kid activities to do. I walked back into the room ten minutes later and, I kid you not, one of them was doing a geography puzzle about where the countries of Africa are located, and one of them was reading a book about inventions across history.

You heard me. I leaned out of parenting (or what my kids think parenting is, entertaining them) and now my kids are better people.

Motherhood:
All ~~love~~ *exhaustion* begins and ends there.

ROBERT BROWNING

Choose Your Own Adventure: Children *Fighting* Edition

You hear the sound of kids arguing in the next room. It's some crazy-ass bullshit that doesn't even matter, like who gets to play with some toy next, who didn't apologize promptly for accidentally bumping someone, or whether the benefits of a more progressively graduated tax rate would ultimately outweigh the potential pitfalls, both economically and ethically.

You know, normal annoying kid stuff.

The argument is escalating. Yelling is either about to happen or in progress. You have two choices.

The two things you can do when your kids fight:

a.) *Go into the next room and resolve their conflict* using your superior adult intellect and supreme parenting authority. Truly understand who was right and who was wrong, comfort the ill-used and punish the offenders with just, proportionate, and kind discipline.

b.) *Ignore them.* Keep listening for sounds of physical struggle/injury or mandatory "must intervene" nastiness. But overall, let it play out. Keep reading your book and eating your bonbons with your feet up in a perfect stance of relaxation, as you, a parent, were surely doing.

If you chose b, you can look forward to a wondrous future of independent, well-adjusted kids.

If you chose a, go back and read the choices again. Each time you choose a, keep going back and rereading the choices. Because every time you solve a problem for kids, those little weasels are going to ask you to do it again.*

There are exceptions to every rule. Sometimes you have to intervene because it's the only way to get them to quiet down and grant you some peace. Sometimes leaning in actually is leaning out.

The **Lean In** That Pays **Dividends** in Leaning *the Fuck* **Out**

It's key to your sanity and overall wellness to find little windows of kid-free time. So if you invest in any parenting priority, I recommend tricking the kids into thinking sleep is awesome and important.

> Having kids who are asleep is the closest thing to *not* having kids.

Most people who know me have noticed I'm relatively laid-back about parenting. If my kids aren't bothering me, I'm unlikely to intervene in how they're choosing to use their time. With my history of lax discipline, it often comes as a surprise to friends and family that I have strictly enforced bedtime from the moment my kids started sleeping through the night.

Usually I feel like I can't get my kids to do anything I want them to do. I've told my kids to say "please" and "thank you" 75,000 times and they still don't do it without prompting. That's not exaggerating for humor's sake—that's just an actual statistic. But I succeeded in getting them to be cool about bedtime.

There are two possible approaches to getting your kids to go the fuck to sleep. The first is a leaning in approach:

Approach A

Make bedtime the most important thing in your life. Leave fun parties early to get the kids to bed. Carry blackout fabric and thumbtacks to vacation houses; after check-in, spend the first forty minutes sun-proofing the kids' room, as if they are vampires. Set an alarm on your phone that goes off at a very early hour (6:30 p.m.? Maybe 7:00?), and whatever's happening at that time must be dropped immediately to get the kids to bed. Tell babysitters, "Let them do whatever they want as long as you have them in bed on time." Any kid who gets out of bed for a nonemergency receives a simple consequence: Their bedtime is twenty minutes earlier the next day.

Approach A is a little fucking much, so it wouldn't be my favorite. But it can lead to a solid amount of well-earned couch time at the end of long days of parenting. This could be a short-term lean in that leads to a long-term lean the fuck out.

The second approach is a little more laid-back and still can lead to long windows of child-free time.

Approach B

#*1* Don't make a big deal about anything being important . . . EXCEPT

#*2* Make a really big fucking deal about bedtime being important.

Because kids are constantly bombarded by demands about how to be and what to do, it makes sense that they resist a lot of it. That's how I'd respond: If someone asked me to do 1,000 things a day, I'd probably bat about .250 on completing them.

But if they asked me to do one thing, I would be sure to get a perfect score.

Give your kids a lot of control over their day and autonomy to choose things. But never bedtime. Bedtime is sacred.

You can tell the kids it's because of their health and well-being, which is partially true. But you'll know the truth:

They need to go the fuck to sleep so you can return to something resembling sanity and consider your own dormant needs for a blessed moment.

That said, if you have one of those kids who won't sleep, first of all, I see you and I love you. Hang the fuck in there.

Second, it's not your fault—you didn't do anything wrong. Some kids go through a short phase or an epically long phase where they refuse sleep. Lean the fuck out of trying to figure out "what you did wrong" when the answer is absolutely nothing.

And third, this won't last forever. The worst part is not that the kid won't sleep, it's the feeling that this phase will never end. It will!

I am excited for you that someday it will be different and you can more fully enjoy the ultimate parenting lean out: children who are asleep.

Time to Unsubscribe

Do you ever feel like you don't have enough time to be as good a parent as you'd like? Guess what—you probably don't! This is not a personal failing, it's a social problem. Work schedules are not designed to accommodate parenthood. School funding is inadequate to supply free before-school and after-school care. These are structural problems—not *you* problems! So unsubscribe from the bullshit concept that you can do it all as a parent—without any help from schools, your boss, your spouse, or your community.

Haters Gonna Hate

Becoming a parent is the shortest path to having everyone in the world believe you're doing everything wrong. Out of nowhere appears a whole army of people you didn't even know existed: people who think it's their God-given right to share, or, more often, passive-aggressively imply, all their criticisms.

In the Gene Wilder movie *Willy Wonka & the Chocolate Factory*—yes, the one that haunted your dreams as a child because Violet eats a stick of forbidden gum and is turned into a giant blueberry—one of the Oompa Loompa songs features the following audacious verse:

Who do you blame when your kid is a brat,
Pampered and spoiled like a Siamese cat?
Blaming the kids is a lie and a shame.
You know exactly who's to blame:

The mother and the father

On one hand, this film came out in 1971, so even though it comes out anti-cat and probably vaguely racist for calling out Siamese cats specifically, and even though this is pretty heteronormative in its assumption that children are raised by different-gendered couples, I have to give it some credit for laying blame on both the mother *and* the father.

But I notice the mother is listed first. Then as now, the mother tends to be blamed a lot more harshly for a bratty kid.

Is your kid having a temper tantrum? Wow, a good mom would have taught her children how to manage their big feelings by now. Wait, now is your kid *not* throwing a temper tantrum? What the fuck have you been doing, oppressing your children's displays of emotion and making them afraid of feelings?

That's right, you're a subpar parent whether your kid is melting down or not.

Unless you're a dad. Then you are going to get a lot of credit just for knowing the name of your kid.

If you're a man parenting in public without a spouse around, you're likely to get carried around triumphantly on the shoulders of any passersby, or nominated for a Nobel Peace Prize.

But whether you're an overpraised dad or an over-blamed mom, chances are you're doing the world's hardest job in the face of the world's harshest criticism. And a lot of that criticism gets internalized, so that even if there's no one out there directly condemning our parenting, we're still criticizing ourselves.

I had the distinct privilege of watching a youth soccer game recently, and one of the little six-year-olds didn't want to play—as is inevitable. He stood in his little cleats and shin guards and cried until the merciful coach noticed and took him out.

The poor little guy's parents, who happened to be sitting next to me, spent the rest of the (blessedly short) game deconstructing their own parenting. What could they have done differently to avoid these tears?

"Maybe we shouldn't have invited your mom and sister. Maybe that stressed him out."

"Yeah. I told him to get out there and score a goal. Did he think that was too much pressure?"

"Mm-hmm. You know what, he's only seen professional soccer on TV. Maybe we should show him some videos of kids playing soccer. That way, he knows it's just an ordinary thing for kids to do."

"Good idea. And maybe we can ask his cousin to talk to him about it? She plays soccer for the high school."

"Shoot, we should have asked her to talk to him before this game. I forgot."

"Maybe we don't invite the grandparents next week. So it's less of a crowd for him."

And so on. These poor parents were leaning in to parenting so hard, they forgot that sometimes six-year-olds just bug out for no reason. With no intervention, he'd probably be fine by the next week. Or the week after.

Or, better yet, possibly they have received the gift of a child who will never like soccer. This will save them hundreds of rec league dollars and thousands of tedious minutes watching youth soccer.

Next time you hear external or internal criticism of your parenting, lean all the way the fuck out of that noise. You're doing a great job.

Be There-*ish* for Your Kids

When you realize that you can't win at parenting, especially in the eyes of others, it actually takes the pressure off. You are raising children in an age when parents are regularly criticized—even for being *too* good.

It's often said that "helicopter parents" hover around their kids too much, performing too many tasks for them and micromanaging their daily lives and long-term plans. "Snowplow parents" clear the path in front of the child to ensure they don't encounter any difficulties. Both of these varieties of "evil," too-good parents are supposedly preventing their kids from developing their own independence and resilience.

Before you let anyone make you feel bad for being a helicopter or a snowplow or whatever cool vehicle you're supposed to avoid being, take a step back and ask: Why would I lean toward hyper-involvement in the first place?

It's definitely not the easiest choice for a full-time working mom. Or for any parent.

Chances are, you've been privy to the research that shows children who have strong parental involvement in their lives are more likely to grow up happy and healthy and successful. You've also been exposed to a culture where attachment parenting is encouraged from the moment a baby is born, where toys are all meant to be purposeful and educationally enriching, where playdates are to be arranged to develop social skills, where signing your kids up for several sports from the time they can kick a ball is an expectation. In fact, some who read my advice to let your kids argue with each other, stop entertaining them, and generally leave them the fuck alone might wonder: Wouldn't I then be neglecting my children?

"Holy shit!" a parent's brain goes. "If I don't hover around my kids nonstop, they will be seven times more likely to develop asthma! They will develop trust issues and fail to learn the ability to self-regulate! Their life expectancy will be reduced by 2.8 years! I'd better buy them some LEGOs and suffer through assembling them together!"

Other times, parenting feels like a competition. With Maddy's dad packing dehydrated seaweed chips in her lunch (which she *loves* and *eats all of*!) and Aiden's mom volunteering to organize the Parent's Surprise Storytime Reader Week, it's easy to worry that things aren't going to turn out okay for your kid and his smushed Hostess cupcakes and mom who forgot (again) which day she signed up to be the damn surprise reader.

But the truth beyond these conflicting pressures is that there is a happy medium.

> *It's good for parents to be involved in their kids' life—but it's not good for parents to be stuck to their kids like quick-dry sparkle glue twenty-four hours a day.*

Sure, it's important to be there for your kids. But being there can mean, you know, there-ish. Like in the next room. Sipping a margarita with a little umbrella in it—okay, more likely, planning a family vacation or paying bills or checking homework or mapping out a career move, but do the umbrella margarita whenever possible—while the kids figure out ways to troubleshoot and problem-solve and entertain themselves for once.

Instead of us all struggling to be a perfect parent, well aware that there are pitfalls on both sides of helicoptering versus ignoring, let's split the difference. Never a helicopter, but maybe occasionally you indulge in parenting like one of those tiny drones that sound like a buzzing bee. Mostly, though, you can step back and let your kids do their thing whenever feasible.

And the spare time and energy you save by not being a perfect parent? You can use it to relax. Proceed directly to Chapter 7 for ideas on how to make your life fulfilling when you're no longer micromanaging your kids.

Behind every
young child
who believes
in himself
is a parent who
~~believed first.~~ left them the fuck alone

MATTHEW L. JACOBSON

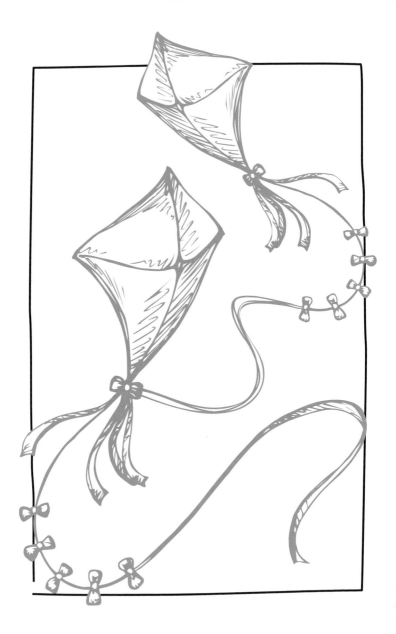

Chapter 6

Things to *Care* Less About

On top of the huge, time-consuming, soul-sucking pressures we put on ourselves, like achieving every thing at work and at home, there are a fuck-ton of little pressures, too. Sometimes I feel like I'm playing Pokémon, constantly bumping up against tiny worries and responsibilities and collecting and nurturing each and every one. Gotta catch 'em all!

Anybody who's seen the animated movie *Encanto* (2021) knows it's a perfect analogy for modern life's overemphasis on leaning in. Everyone in town is depending on the Madrigals, the magical talented family, to do everything perfectly. Many of us feel like a combination of all the Madrigal women: We need to stay strong and carry all the burdens like Luisa, make everything beautiful and well decorated like Isabela, listen to everyone and stay broadly aware like Dolores, feed and heal everyone like Julieta, and control our emotions and maintain a placid exterior like Pepa. All the while, we might feel like Mirabel, with no particular talents or gifts.

But, both film and real-life spoiler alert: We don't actually need to do everything perfectly. This chapter will offer a smorgasbord of smaller things you can let slide right off your plate.

I promise the world will continue to turn.

Being the *Fun* <u>One</u>

"I'm the funniest one in the family," my adorable little six-year-old son claimed. "Then Daddy's the second funniest. Then my sister. Then Mommy. Mommy's the least funny."

"Do you know that MOMMY is a professional joke writer?" I bellowed. "Do you know that STRANGERS frequently contact MOMMY and say, 'Thank you, your article made me laugh and brightened my day'? Do you know that I don't even think it's funny when you make fart noises with your mouth? That I'm just fake laughing to be nice?!?"

I mean, this is what I said in my mind. But I'm not the fun one, so in real life I just said, "Okay, bud."

I've heard so many of my friends claim some version of "I'm not the fun one." This claim is especially prevalent among those of the "women in relationships with men" variety. Maybe you always volunteer to be the designated driver, or you're usually the first one to get tired during a big night out. Maybe your guy friends always have fun poker nights or guys' weekends, and you have trouble getting those together with your girlfriends. Maybe your spouse is the one who's "good at" playing with the kids, but you're "not a good player."

We're so accustomed to being hard on ourselves, we're even hard on ourselves about not being good at having a good time.

I used to teach at an elite college, the kind where you can have straight As and perfect test scores but still not get in. When I first started there, a colleague told me to watch out for a certain kind of student, usually a woman, who was partying way too much, at the brink of falling apart.

"Won't it be easy to tell who they are?" I asked. "Won't I notice their grades slipping, or see that they're missing class?"

"Oh no," my coworker laughed. "They won't miss a day of class. Their papers will still be perfect."

"I wouldn't expect these nerdy valedictorian types to be big partyers," I remember saying. Throughout my career as a college teacher, I have seen that alcohol and drugs are the easiest, surest, quickest way for a student facing no other challenges to destroy their academic careers. I'd assumed that kids who'd already accomplished so much wouldn't fall prey to such a typical demise.

"It's not enough for them to be perfect academically," my coworker explained. "They're also trying to be perfect socially. They're trying to win at partying."

Somewhere along the line, in addition to the serious business of making sure our careers and households were being run flawlessly, we also started to put pressure on ourselves to be riotously fun, hilariously joyful barrels of laughs.

To the women who think they're not fun enough, I say, first of all, I bet you're more fun than you think. There's more than one way to be fun, and not every kind of fun involves staying up all night and jumping up on the bar singing along to Lizzo, or wrestling with the kids when clearly the coffee table is right there just waiting for an adorable little noggin to get a big bump on it.

Give yourself a break and recognize that you contribute joy in subtler but equally valuable ways.

But also: Did you ever consider that maybe the reason you're "not the fun one" is because you're . . .[gestures wildly at the whole rest of this book]?

It's hard to be fun when you're carrying the weight of the world on your shoulders.

Who has time for fun—or the inclination to let go and be silly—when you're taking on extra tasks at work, cooking healthy gourmet meals, keeping your house neat and tastefully decorated, remembering to pay the bills and mail

When life gives you lemons, make lemonade.^

—MODERN PROVERB

or, you know, throw out the lemons and just buy whatever drink you want the birthday cards and sign the report cards and send in snacks for the PTA meeting, calling the plumber, practicing self-care, posting photos on social media that show how amazing your life is, saving the Earth by knowing whether it's better to drink seltzer from a plastic bottle or cans, and in sum doing every fucking thing?

You might need to lean the fuck out of a bunch of things before you can lean in to fun.

And of course, stop giving a fuck whether you're the fun one.

Weight

I have two cats. They were born in the same litter, they've lived with me since they were born, and they look exactly alike. *Exactly* alike. You know how some cats have little markings that make them different from their twin sisters? Not mine. Even their markings are identical. I feed them at the same time, exactly measured food that is the same for each of them, and they get pretty much the same level of activity. There's just one difference between them: Mango is tiny. Clementine is gigantic.

Their bodies process food and movement in completely different ways.

People are no different. Two people can be equally healthy and weigh different amounts. It's high time we put an end to the number on the scale being a stand-in for our overall health—and a proxy for our self-worth.

I'm sending out advance apologies for what I'm about to admit, because I'm not proud of it. But here's the truth: I've wasted a lot of time and energy in my life (1) worrying about not being thin enough and (2) feeling annoyed with and envious of people, especially fellow women, who are skinny.

I know, I know! I said I'm not proud of it.

But over the years, I started to notice a few surprising facts. First, I started to notice that no matter how I looked or felt, there always seemed to be some nearby weight horizon that I couldn't reach. I'd think to myself, "I mean, I'm fine with my weight, of course I'm body-positive, and I don't buy into all this dieting culture bullshit. But still, it would be great to lose five pounds." Five pounds later, it would seem like a good idea to lose five more pounds.

I once lost so much weight my organs stopped functioning. That's my sort of dramatic but medically accurate way of saying I stopped getting my period for a few months. I'll give you a single guess whether, at that time, I was satisfied by the appearance of my body.

Reader, you guessed right. I still was not.

And it wasn't just me. I had grown up with the notion that skinny was the goal. But I had lots of skinny friends—I mean, really slender people—and they also seemed to find ways to be dissatisfied with their bodies. I have a thin friend who thinks her shoulders are too . . . whatever it is, it feels so silly to me I forget what it is. I think she thinks her shoulders are too pointy. I have a couple of skinny friends who worry they are *too* skinny, a concern that has many different manifestations, most commonly a concern that their boobs or their butts are inadequately small. I have a friend whose concern is that her calves are too slender in proportion to her ankles (or that her ankles are too wide compared to her slender calves, or both). I distinctly remember a girl in high school who was very thin, and there was a cute little fold of skin right in front of her armpit, between her arm and her boob, that she didn't like. She thought it looked fat.

I gathered all these factoids, used all my brilliant powers of Sherlock Holmes–style deduction, and came to an important conclusion:

Something other than our bodies is wrong.

It's the patriarchy that's wrong. (It's always the patriarchy.)

I and all the women I knew were internalizing an ever-growing list of exacting standards about our bodies. Were these standards informational, helping us unlock our attractiveness? In other words, were we unattractive because of our perceived hideous "flaws"—for example, the skin necessary to allow our ball-and-socket shoulder joints the full range of motion, aka the "fat" skin fold my high school classmate found unacceptable?

Of course not!

You are attractive even if you aren't shaped like a Barbie doll—famously so out of proportion that she wouldn't be able to walk if she were a real woman—or her modern equivalent, the Kardashian or influencer of your choice who seems to exist to shove the body positivity movement back thirty years. What people find attractive is idiosyncratic, mysterious, and fun. Body standards don't exist to inform us how to be attractive.

Time to Unsubscribe

Are ads making you feel like you need to work harder at being your already-gorgeous self? Being sold a certain version of beauty is usually a smoke screen for being sold a particular beauty product. Go ahead and unsubscribe from those corporate beauty ideals and make your own rules instead—preferably ones that prioritize soothing spa treatments and doing nothing but embracing your inner beauty.

Body standards exist to keep us worried, to keep us always feeling inadequate, to prevent us from getting ahead and living a satisfied life.

And the only way out is to insist on loving your body. We have to eat and we have to exercise, but the goal of each should be to feel physically good, not to manipulate our weight.

Paunchy waist, short legs, saggy boobs, pointy shoulders— these are all hot.

Time to lean the fuck out of hating the skin between your arm and your torso, and lean in to loving all your skin.

Clothes

I once shared a social circle with a woman who wore a foot-high beehive wig and a brightly colored mod '60s dress every single day. You'd show up to a party with everyone wearing jeans and tees, and she'd always be there with a gorgeous, cherry-red or apple-green sleeveless A-line dress and a glorious pile of hair on her head. I can't remember her name because everyone called her "Beehive." She was stately and inspiring.

But ask me what anyone else in the whole wide world has ever worn on any day of their lives? Beats me. I can't remember

What Might Happen If You Don't Look Good One Day

You're in a hurry and wear a V-neck shirt under a square-neck overall romper; the necklines are objectively not pleasing together. Also the romper is boxy and not too flattering. Let's imagine what might go wrong in your day.

7:45 a.m. – Spouse leaves for work and instead of the usual, "I love you! Have a great day!" you just receive a glance at your outfit and a curt, "Bye."

8:32 a.m. – Someone cuts you off in traffic, and as they pass, they beep and scream, "Your shirts' necklines clash!"

8:33 a.m. – The next driver behind the beeper strains so hard to get a good look at your lousy outfit that they forget to keep an eye on the road. They run a red light right in front of you. Oncoming traffic crashes into the outfit-looker, and the cars behind that one crash into it, leading to an eighteen-car pileup.

This story has a happy ending. ☺

Does everyone survive the wreck? No. Unfortunately, there are heavy casualties caused by your poor clothing choice.

But as the principal eyewitness to the accident and the first person on the scene, you rush ahead to give first aid to the victims. You have no choice but to tear your outfit to shreds in order to dress their wounds. Once all the medical helicopters have taken off from the scene, you're able to turn around and drive back home. You throw away the remaining rags from your unflattering outfit and start the day over again, this time with a passable outfit.

10:45 a.m. – You arrive at work. Your boss wanted to fire you for being late, but when she sees you're a competent dresser, she changes her mind. You receive a promotion.

All day – Everyone keeps being like, "Wow, your clothes are very nice. I like and respect you."

6:15 p.m. – You arrive home. Your spouse is sitting at the dining room table. They look up at you somberly, sadly. Then their eye catches your changed outfit. They reach into the manila envelope in front of them, pull out the papers inside, and tear the documents to pieces. "I was ready to ask you for a divorce, based on your unappealing clothing choice this morning," they say. "But I see you've changed your outfit. Now I'm falling in love with you all over again." They run across the room toward you, take you and your not-ugly outfit in their arms, and kiss you deeply.

the clothing choices of even my very best friends, to whom I've said, "I love your outfit!" a thousand times—and meant it. Yet I have no idea what those beloved outfits were.

Still, every day getting dressed, I scrutinize myself in the mirror as if I'll be going before a panel of judges who will examine me with magnifying glasses and throw rotten tomatoes at my head if I don't reach some level of style and sophistication.

In truth, no one is likely to notice what anyone besides the cool beehive lady is wearing. And if they do notice, they'll forget momentarily.

If you love choosing clothing carefully and staying on the edge of fashion, keep at it! Lean right on in.

But if you agonize or worry about what you're wearing, time to let that one go. You look hot. If you don't, it doesn't matter as much as you think. What I loved about Beehive's look was not the clothes themselves, but her audacity at wearing them. No matter what you have on, confidence makes it look smashing.

 *Stop* Trying to Single-Handedly Save the Earth

If we could bottle up the energy we're spending worrying about the tiny details of our own liability for climate change, we'd be able to solve climate change.

Now, listen. I'm not saying stop giving a damn about our lovely Mother Earth. She's so pretty! And more importantly, 99 percent of environmentally friendly actions individuals can take to help the environment are super easy.

Saving the Earth shouldn't mean carrying the weight of the Earth on your own shoulders.

In kindergarten, I learned to reduce, reuse, and recycle. Recycling? Easy peasy. I wrote about a hundred drafts of this book, and each time I realized a page wasn't funny and I wanted to crumple it up and throw it in the trash, I would instead crumple it up and throw it into . . . the recycling. You're welcome, trees!

Reusing is easy, too. For example, I am obsessed with and addicted to Mexican food, so I buy a lot of tortillas, which come in a convenient little baggie. When I'm finished with all ten tortillas in the package, which usually takes me about two days, I never, ever throw it out. It's now a plastic baggie, in my plastic baggie rotation. I don't even have to give a single goddamn about the environment to want to reuse that thing. It's a free fucking baggie!

By the way, if you had a weird grandma or auntie who would rinse out baggies, dry them on the drying rack, and reuse them, now might be a good time to apologize to her for thinking she was weird. She was 100 percent right and that was great for the environment. Even if you don't apologize, she's not sweating it: Dolphins love her.

Reducing is the easiest one of all, because it just means doing and using _less._

All you have to do is sit there, and boom, you're reducing. Congrats! Here's your Nobel Prize!

Giving a damn about the environment is completely compatible with being lazy and frugal, which means I can more or less handle it.

Basically, any time you're leaning the fuck out, you're very likely helping the environment.

But the demand to reduce and reuse and recycle can throw some of us into an obsessive tailspin of worry and perfectionism.

Time to Unsubscribe

Climate change needs to be stopped at the policy level—not at the level of you dying of dehydration because you forgot your reusable water bottle and are really thirsty but feel too guilty to buy a plastic one. Feel free to do your part, but don't subscribe to the bullshit notion that the future of the planet rests only on your shoulders.

Picture me, about to rinse out my plastic tortilla baggie so I can reuse it like your weird aunt, but pausing to think, *Wait, is this definitely the most environmentally friendly thing to do? What if I use so much water in rinsing this that I offset the benefits of reducing the plastic in the landfill or ocean? Exactly how much water expenditure is worth saving a small piece of thin plastic from going into the garbage? What if the food gets stuck at the bottom of the baggie, and I have to use some dish soap to clean it, and then I'm buying the dish soap replacement sooner, and that comes in a plastic bottle anyway??* And then going down a thirty-minute internet rabbit hole trying to figure out whether I should rinse out the baggie.

It's time to stop and accept that, on an individual level, a low-key "doing your best" does help the environment and absolutely is enough.

Environmental researchers talk about a concept called "individualization of responsibility," often just referred to as "individualization." The idea of individualization is that when everyone is constantly worried about—and distracted by—their personal responsibility for reducing carbon emissions and avoiding pollution, it's easier for big companies and governments and institutions to ignore the large collective action that would actually help solve the problem in a considerably bigger way. In fact, if you hear companies or governments or big institutions encouraging people to take individual actions to save the Earth, you should be suspicious: They are trying to distract you from what *they* should be doing (often something they don't want to do because it might eat into their profits) to solve the problem at the macro level. Those sneaky bastards.

When I say to worry about the environment less, I'm warning you about the dangers of individualization. Freaking out about every micro decision not only doesn't help the environment much, but it also makes you feel bad when you've done absolutely nothing wrong.

In other words, lean the fuck out of the extra worry about the parts that are out of your hands. Sure, go ahead and do your base-level environmental giving a damn—reduce, reuse, recycle. Then, instead of obsessing about whether all your light bulbs are the right Energy Star rating or whether your social media "friends" have a more pesticide-free garden than you or whether it's more green to buy seltzer in many small cans or a few large plastic bottles, you can throw any time or energy or brain space you have left into demanding businesses and governments enact the broad policies necessary to actually create a sustainable future.

Or, you know, take a nice, lovely nap. It's actually quite environmentally friendly to nap!

Take Things Less *Personally*

My all-time favorite exchange on a TV show is from the HBO drama *Boardwalk Empire*. The protagonist, the Atlantic City politician and gangster Nucky Thompson, played by Steve Buscemi, is chatting with another gangster, Gyp Rosetti, played by Bobby Cannavale. Nucky advises Gyp, "I learned a long time ago not to take things personally."

Gyp responds, "Everyone's a person, though, right? So how else could they take it?"

Now, Gyp Rosetti is not a good role model. He's been killing lots of colleagues, enemies, and strangers over minor perceived slights. He murders someone for saying something he perceived as an insult to his intelligence. Later, he pours gasoline on someone and burns them to death for wishing him good luck. (Gyp doesn't want anyone to wish him good luck because he wants it widely known and understood that he does not need luck. "Good luck" sounds condescending to him.) "What the fuck is life," he later asks, "if it's not personal?"

I have to admit that, aside from the murder-y bits, I can empathize with this murderous fictional gangster.

We move through life perceiving everything through our own eyes, from our own subjective standpoint. So a lot of things that other people do or say can feel pretty fucking personal.

A short list of things you could choose to take personally:

 # 1 When someone you've already met reintroduces themselves, not remembering your first encounter. It can lead to an all-out identity crisis. What, are you not memorable? Do you make such a paltry impression? Or, worse, does Brenda actually remember meeting you but is now waging large-scale psychological warfare, trying and partially succeeding at destroying your suddenly fragile ego?

#2 When someone starts spacing out in the middle of a story you're telling them. A blow nearly impossible to recover from. This is one of your better stories! You cannot be any more entertaining than this! Have you already told this one to Rachel? What would happen if you were telling one of your second-tier stories—would she fall asleep right in front of your face?

Should you crawl into a dark hole and live there forever? Of course not! The truth is actually freeing.

You are not at the center of Brenda's and Rachel's universes.

Maybe Brenda's dog was sick the day she first met you. And maybe Rachel was distracted during your kick-ass story—like her phone was buzzing or her bra was itchy and she was trying not to be weird by reaching under her shirt right in front of you.

The point is, most people do things and say things for reasons that are personal—but they're personal to them. They rarely have anything to do with you.

If you need inspiration for taking things less personally, go to a crowded community pool on a hot day and watch the kids play for half an hour.

There's not nearly enough room in the pool for all the wild playing these kids want to do. They are constantly bumping into each other, kicking each other, splashing waves of water into each other's faces. Have you ever been bumped into, kicked, or splashed in a pool? It's extremely fucking annoying.

So a kid will get kicked in the face. That kick in the face will be followed by a full minute of being splashed in their face that was just kicked. And that poor kicked and splashed kid will look around in pure, unadulterated rage, with a face that simultaneously says, "What. The. Fuck?" and "I'm out for blood." She can't believe the injustice that's just occurred.

And then, after looking around for a second, she spots the offender: some other little kid who's swimming away.

And it dawns on her: Oh, that kid wasn't trying to hurt me or bother me at all. She's just swimming over to the pool ladder because her mom said it's time to go to the snack bar. And she's not very coordinated, so she accidentally kicked me, and she didn't realize I was right behind her so her swim kicks splashed me.

It has _nothing_ to do with me.

And the kid who just got kicked and splashed in the face turns back around and resumes her joyful swim.

So don't take Gyp Rosetti as your role model. Take a little kid at the community pool. She's your hero. Because she came to the right conclusion:

It has nothing to do with me.

<u>Stop</u> Trying to Be
a *Perfect* Feminist

I once witnessed a twenty-minute argument between two brilliant women about whether wearing mascara is compatible with feminism.

Even as someone who loves debates, loves women, wears mascara but sometimes wonders whether makeup is a concession to the patriarchy, believes in equality for all people, and wants to be a good feminist, I found this conversation painful. It was like watching sailors on a sinking ship argue whether to boil or fry the eggs for tomorrow's breakfast. We have more important matters at hand, shipmates!

To worry less about being a perfect feminist, you don't need to stop caring about equal rights for all genders. You can keep caring about women and equality, and you can keep doing whatever you do in your life that you think advances equality.

To worry less about feminism, you can simply let yourself stop micro-analyzing every aspect of your daily life. Stop measuring yourself against some unclear standards of perfect gender neutrality. Stop beating yourself up if you occasionally find yourself falling into a gender stereotype.

Stop considering whether mascara is good or bad for women. Just wear mascara if you want to and don't if you don't.

Things You're Allowed to Do Even If They're Not Perfectly Feminist

✫ Really, really, deeply care which bachelorette ends up with the guy.

✫ Buy gifts for yourself for your birthday. Wrap them in nice wrapping paper. Open them in the presence of your significant other or children and say, "Wow, omg, thank you!" even though they didn't do shit.

✫ Volunteer to take notes at the work meeting. Sure, this is the type of menial office labor that was relegated to women in the old days, so some might find it demeaning. But sometimes you just want to lean the fuck out at a work meeting and still look like you're doing something.

✫ Decline a promotion. The lean-in ideology might condemn this as anti-feminist, but not every job advancement is right for every woman.

✫ Like sports. Or don't. Whatevs. You don't need to subvert gender expectations by pretending to care about the trade deadline or the playoffs or the play deadline or the trade-offs. But if you need to fake liking sports to impress someone who likes sports . . . go right ahead! Pretend to care who scores so you can score.

✫ Feel jealous of other women. Yes, we are all in this together. But damn, sometimes it's just frustrating when it seems like Sarah is having all the success and also her teeth are so damn white and straight and she never seems to accidentally leave the house in a shirt that has a more conspicuous stain than you remembered like you did Tuesday.

✪ Bake the cookies for the work potluck or PTA bake sale. Yes, this book has a whole chapter about leaning the fuck out of cooking. But sometimes, with your favorite music blasting and a pact with yourself to let all other obligations fuck off, a couple of winter hours in front of a warm oven can be therapeutic. Plus, you get to eat spoonfuls of raw cookie dough the whole time.

My point is, yes, there's a minimum level of caring about living a feminist life that everyone—no matter their gender identity—should be invested in. Living an equitable life, in which you're not pigeonholed into certain tasks or personalities based on your gender, is really fucking important.

But that doesn't mean we have to police the intricacies of our personal lives to make sure we're always meeting the standard.

You occasionally perform some tediously gender-predictable task?

Lean the fuck out of self-judgment for that!

Chapter 7

Things to Care More About, Like *Happiness*

So far, this book has been about things you can and should drop out of your life. And if you're following all the advice, you may have noticed you're worrying, cooking, parenting, working, cleaning, and generally wasting your time with bullshit way less. Great job leaning out!

With all this nonsense off your plate, you may realize that you now have a moment to stop and think about yourself for a change.

You can consider what makes you happy, what you want your life to be about. You may even be able to think about the ways you want to fix the system so that it's not so difficult for all of us to get the space we need and deserve.

So many of us, especially women, have been taught that the bullshit *is* life, that we should be deriving meaning from slogging through the dismal thankless duties of our day-to-day. Where does meaning come from, if not from worrying about all the little tasks and expectations imposed upon us? And when we stop allowing the most dismal duties to fill our time and dictate our self-worth, what's left to define our lives?

Lots of wonderful things! Let's explore all the beautiful options together.

Spend *More* Time
with Friends

I've occasionally heard people claim that college is the best time of a person's life, and I'm always skeptical. Sure, it was fun, it was interesting, but it comes at a rough time in life—before you know what you want to do and what you care about and who you are, before you have financial and emotional stability, but after you've left the care of your childhood home.

Then I remember: For many people, college was the one time in life when they lived in a walkable community with convenient amenities and constant access to the company of peers.

Aside from a few sunny exceptions—school, summer camp, prison—we're rarely surrounded by peers. Without a bunch of them within easy reach, it often takes a great deal of work to start and maintain relationships with peers. Plus, the more worries and responsibilities and duties we accumulate throughout life—frankly, the more bullshit on our plates—the less energy we have, and the less inclined we often feel to do that "work" of hanging out with friends.

My parents used to have so many stories about a particular friend of theirs from the old days, and they obviously both had so much love for this dude. I finally asked them, "How come you don't still hang out with Paul?"

They looked sort of puzzled, trying to piece together what happened. "He would come over our house to hang out like he always did, but we'd always be rushing off to your basketball practices or dance recitals or whatever," they explained. "Eventually he just . . . stopped coming."

Now this was a shitty thing for my parents to say, as it essentially accused my existence of wrecking their social lives and overall well-being. But the point is valid:

When you lean in to being the perfect employee and the perfect spouse and the perfect parent and the perfect homemaker, you risk leaning out of the soul-sustaining friendships that allow you to embrace your imperfections.

The time and energy you put into leaning in can foreclose on the possibility of making new friendships.

And it doesn't help that many friends and would-be friends are in essentially the same boat as you. So even when you do pry yourself away from your job(s) and chores and reach out to make or maintain a friendship, sometimes you get rebuffed by another frazzled leaner-inner who's trying to do too much and doesn't have time for your bright idea to have a nice little chat over a latte, or go backcountry survival camping in grizzly-infested woods, or whatever it is friends like to do for fun.

So, how can a desperately busy person whose network is full of other desperately busy people actually spend meaningful time with friends?

☆ *Fake like your teeth are horrible.* If you have the kind of flexible job where you can leave in the middle of the day to go to the dentist, occasionally just leave to get coffee with your friend. And say you're going to the dentist. What's going on in my mouth, whether it's a root canal or a muffin and a vanilla latte, is none of Lisa in HR's business.

☆ *Buy or make gifts for people.* Seriously, when you're super busy, it's hard to come up with reasons you need to see your friends; working overtime and shuttling kids to soccer and redoing the backsplash or whatever can take up all our time and attention. But damn, when you're like, "I have a tiny gift for you! Really it's nothing, just a trifle. Can I come over and drop it off this week?" the schedules clear. Bonus: Then they might feel a little pressure to buy or make something for you. Think of it as an investment in yourself.

☆ *Be persistent.* Not everyone has reached your level of enlightenment. Give them this book, and then when they get to this exact bullet point on this exact page, they'll realize how foolish it is to neglect friendship and human company in the interest of all the other bullshit we've been told to worry about. Suddenly *they'll* be begging *you* to hang out.

You've got friends who, deep down in their hearts, want to see you, but these adorable bitches will put you off indefinitely because they're leaning in and they're technically "busy" all the time.

Pretty much every study on happiness ever conducted has concluded that cultivating relationships is the key to human joy and contentment. So you can feel free to lean out of everything else—but make sure you don't lean the fuck out of friends and family and even your more casual acquaintances. Even little chats with work peeps and primary care doctors and your local café's barista have big potential to supply joy, and leaning the fuck out of all the worries discussed in the previous chapters leaves room for those revitalizing relationships.

Sleep More

The medical community agrees: Sleep is listed as a prevention or cure for basically anything that can go wrong with your mind or body.

The other great news? Sleep feels awesome.

This combination of facts is like finding out you have a disease and you can cure it by eating more chocolate.

Here is an incomplete list of
the greatest pleasures in life:

☆ Lying down in bed when you're really tired.

☆ Taking a random li'l nap in the middle of the day.

☆ Lying down on the couch while someone else is watching something really boring on TV, like golf.

☆ Dozing off, under any circumstances.

☆ Suddenly waking up, realizing it's not time to get up yet, and falling back asleep.

In short, we are being told that one of the most enjoyable things ever is also really good for us. That never happens!

Yet, we still don't sleep enough. The CDC says that more than a third of American adults regularly don't get a healthy night's sleep. Even more shocking: A somewhat less scientific study of people I know reports that 100 percent of adults don't get enough sleep.

Go the fuck to bed, people!

It's the coziest place in your house. (Note: You may need to lean the fuck out of a bunch of other stuff before you have enough time to follow this order.)

Dump More

This advice has nothing to do with poop. I'm sure that however often you're doing those kinds of dumps is just fine. If you have concerns about your defecation schedule, please seek medical attention.

Instead, I'd like to gently propose that you break up with people more.

The woman who needs to read this book likes to keep her head down and work hard, and sometimes she can be pretty hard on herself.

For a career, maybe that's fine. I don't know anything about careers: I'm over here writing a humor book, so you should take job advice from people who have made better career decisions than writing a book full of swear words.

But I'm positive that our tendency to "keep your head down, work hard, and be hard on yourself" is a terrible way to approach relationships.

When we work really hard and maybe are constantly working on ourselves, it makes it feel okay and normal when the person we're dating is also hard on us. We might not notice little insults. Or when we do, they feel deserved.

You have

ignore or reject

to ~~kiss~~

a lot of frogs

before you find

your prince.

—MODERN PROVERB

*Please, note
you don't owe
any frogs
or any princes
any kisses.*

But I'm going to whisper an important little simple nugget of wisdom that would have saved me a lot of heartache if I had realized it a little sooner: [whispers] Whoever you're dating should be nice to you.

It's basically the main job of a romantic partner to be nice to you. Not every now and then, when they're apologizing or want to make out. All the fucking time.

Much as I would like to, I can't tell you what to look for in a dating partner. People are weird and we all like different things, and that's the beauty of it. I once had a roommate who told me the most important trait she looked for in a dating partner was a good sense of style. Like, if you are any person with any looks and any personality, Krista will date you—if you have the right cut of trousers and your asymmetrical haircut falls across your forehead in an aesthetically pleasing way. To me, that's an odd priority. But who cares? I don't have to date Krista's significant others. (Although I did once. Don't tell Krista.)

But what I hope my roommate could have nudged into the #1 spot of dating priorities, just one notch above "doesn't wear sports jerseys to parties," would be "is really nice to me all the time." I wish she had said to me, "The most important thing I look for in a person to date is that they're really nice to me all the time. Second most important is that they can pull off black-and-white wingtip vintage dancing shoes."

People are reluctant to dump their mean partners because it's scary out there, being single. Once I told my mom I had broken up with one boyfriend or another, and she cried, *"Why?!"* To this day, she claims she said that because she thought we'd been so happy together. (We weren't.) But I'm pretty sure I detected the faint whiff of desperation in her question. The question behind the question "Why?" was, "How do you know someone else is going to come along?" And the concern behind the question behind the question was, "Who's going to love this weird daughter of mine next? Anyone? *Any*one?"

That fear can make it seem like it's a good idea to just stick it out with the person who's here right now.

The old expression goes, a bird in the hand is worth two in the bush, right?

No fucking way.

A bird in the hand is terrible if it's pecking at you. Maybe one of those bush birds won't peck you. Let that mean bird in your hand go.

I always hear anecdotes about "ultimatums." According to the ultimatum story, some person, usually the woman in a hetero-sexual relationship, demands a marriage proposal by such and such a date. If the other person, usually the man in a heterosexual relationship, doesn't propose by then, she breaks up with him.

Can we make a social pact to avoid letting it get to that? If you're with someone who insults you by stringing you along in a way that makes you unhappy, dump them. Then, you'll never have to beg this mean person to marry you.

In other words, dump more!

Ask for *What You Want* More

We were standing side by side in the ocean when my eight-year-old suddenly said, "I just put my head underwater! Compliment me!"

"Great job putting your head underwater!" I said, very uncertain why this amounted to a compliment-worthy achievement.

"Thanks," she said. Then she paused before adding, "Even though I asked for the compliment, it still counts."

It took some piecing together, but I figured out why my daughter so deeply believed she deserved praise that she specifically asked for it. The water was cold and she didn't want to put her head under, so this was a feat of bravery. And, she'd noticed that her younger brother, who was just learning to swim, had been garnering a lot of attention and praise for doing simple in-water tasks like submerging his head. So she wanted to get in on that action. She wanted me to notice her fortitude and skill.

I started to dream about going around all day demanding compliments (which are exactly what I want all the time). I'll set dinner down on the table, waiting expectantly before everyone takes a bite and I'll pounce: "I cooked that! Compliment me!"

I'll hand out my class's next writing assignment, then say, "Students, I know you don't want to do this project, but isn't it a nicely designed assignment? I spent hours on it. Compliment me!"

I'll walk up to strangers on the street and say, "Did you see this outfit that I picked out today? Compliment me!"

A lot of times, we don't get what we want because nobody knows what we want.

As my daughter knows, getting what you want still counts if you ask for it.

(Re)Discover What You Actually Enjoy Doing

A friend of mine recently had a day off from work, and when I asked him what he was going to do with his free time, he paused. Then he paused longer. Finally, he said, "I'll probably end up catching up on some work. What else is there to do?"

Hmm, I wonder if this answer might be gendered. Men have been acculturated to fill their spare time with income-generating labor. I, on the other hand, who have been socialized to take responsibility for domestic space, have sometimes caught myself thinking, "Yay! A spare moment! I can finally dust off the mantel and clean the bathroom mirrors!"

But my dude friend and I share a woeful trait:

We're so alienated from our own leisure, we've forgotten how the hell to enjoy ourselves.

Taking responsibility for work, both in and out of the household, is a necessary part of life, for sure. And the great news is, it can bring satisfaction along with it—we've provided! We're doing a good job! Maybe we even find the work inherently enjoyable!

But because it can sometimes be satisfying, coupled with the fact that it takes up a shit-ton of our time and energy, labor can infiltrate our entire lives. And suddenly, poof, all the neural pathways that used to bring us from boredom to satisfaction and fulfillment are taken over by the "work, and only work, to get fulfillment" connection.

Or, worse yet, shuttled straight from school pressures to work pressures, we never even had a chance to discover what, other than work, gives us satisfaction.

You may be suffering from leisure amnesia—the disease that results when the work part of your brain has overtaken the fun part of your brain.

Symptoms of leisure amnesia include:

☆ not having any hobbies

☆ laughing maniacally when someone asks if you have any hobbies

☆ responding "Does laundry count?" when someone asks if you have any hobbies

☆ googling "What are some examples of hobbies a normal person would have?"

Of course, this aspect of the disease needs no cure: You don't owe the world any conspicuous leisure, and you don't need to cultivate hobbies so you can seem like a cool hobby-haver.

But that said, having activities you like to do other than chores and work is actually important for your well-being. It's well worth leaning in to.

The first place to look for what you enjoy doing is the past.

Yes, now your life is a joyless parade of inane required tasks, but think back: Were you ever previously interested in things?

No one can ever believe this about me because all I do now is hide indoors reading and writing, but when I was young, I was a complete jock. I played every sport and loved basketball especially. And you know what? On the rare occasions I manage to drag my nerdy butt onto a basketball court, I still love it.

Why should children, whose lives are already pretty fun, also get all the fun extracurricular activities? Dust off your flute or paintbrushes or field hockey stick; reteach yourself "Hot Cross Buns" or take a stab at a still life or smash a field hockey ball with that stick and release some aggression.

Having one little hobby revival can sometimes lead to an all-out hobby awakening. After a couple of months of alone, at-home fluting or painting or hockeying, you may find yourself joining the adult field hockey team at the rec center, or contributing badass flute solos to a friend's rock band, or selling your paintings at the farmers' market—or better yet, giving them away to friends, as a little emotional blackmail to force them to hang out with you more. Win-win!

As a kid, being good at those hobbies may have mattered to you. One of the true glories of being a grown-up is . . . it doesn't matter whether you're good at your hobbies. The joy is in taking a break from work to do them.

Now that the pressure to lean in is off the table, you might even consider actively seeking out things you already know you're terrible at. I'm bad at baking, but you know what the consequence is? I end up with various combinations of butter, sugar, and flour that look like messy lumps of disfigured baking nightmares straight out of a Tim Burton movie. They're so ugly that I am not inclined to share them with anyone—but again, they are combinations of butter, sugar, and flour, so they taste amazing. I get these hideous cakes and cookies all to myself.

I also can't draw. I can't even conceptualize how to force my hand to make lines that resemble real-life objects. I'd always heard that drawing was therapeutic, but I never tried it because I have been traumatized by personally ruining so many games of Pictionary. But then my kids had Zoom kindergarten art class, and I was bored enough to try the lessons with them. It was the loveliest calming experience—and a lesson in doing things just because they're inherently enjoyable, not because I'm hoping to get some product or results at the end.

I mean, there were *some* results. If you knew me at that time, your birthday card was definitely a hand-drawn zebra with wobbly stripes and a disproportionately small head. But I took up drawing *mostly* just for fun.

Put *More* Leisure
on Your Calendar

Once you figure out what you like doing, you'll (re)discover the perhaps unfamiliar sensation of enjoyment. And once you get good at enjoying yourself, leaning the fuck out will start to come a little more naturally, because you won't be equating your self-worth with work accolades or domestic feats.

Old habits die hard, though. You're still likely to be busy.

On any given day, you might find yourself occasionally leaning in—and that's okay! You're also leaning the fuck out of beating yourself up for leaning in.

The truth about fun and leisure, when you're a typical adult, is that you can't wait for it to happen. It will rarely happen

Hobbies for Grown-Ups Who No Longer Need to Be Good at Shit

Try gardening. Did you know that if you plant something, and it doesn't grow, there are absolutely no consequences? If you succeed at gardening, you have food to eat or pretty flowers and leaves to decorate your home. If you fail, absolutely nothing bad happens. You go back to the garden store and buy a couple of new plants or seeds.

Try sewing. If you succeed, you can fix those hanging hems, actually replace missing buttons, maybe even design and make your own cool clothes. If you fail, whatevs. You still have a bunch of missing-buttoned blouses accumulating dust in the pile of clothes in your bedroom—just like before!

Try bike riding. You get to see beautiful scenery on the bike trail and get some exercise, which ordinarily sucks, in an unusually fun way. Plus, Leaning Out You is not trying to impress anybody or entering any races, you're just having fun—so you can bike slowly. Like gently, unhurriedly, is-she-even-moving, comically slow.

You miss
100 percent
of the ^*Jell-O* shots
you don't take.

—MODERN PROVERB

spontaneously. Each day is like an empty cup, and work—paid and unpaid—is like a liquid that will take up whatever open space is available. If you don't drop a big rock of leisure into that cup, in advance, the nonleisure time overtakes whatever size and shape receptacle you put it in.

That's why scheduling your leisure is so important. When you're busy and tired, it can sound counterintuitive to be told that the solution is to add more items to your calendar—but truly, this may be the only way to make sure you're making time for yourself.

So, take out your planner. Look at every week, month, and year in that calendar. And make sure every single day has some activities that you actually find fun scheduled in.

Did you just schedule 365 instances of leisure into your next year? Yeah, you did.

You're going to have so much fucking fun this year.

There are (at least) two kinds of leisure. The first kind is passive and mostly involves looking at some screen or another. Scrolling through social media. Flipping through magazines. Watching TV.

This kind of leisure is necessary, because it lets us shut off our brains for a bit. It's the leisure of distraction. To be honest, passive leisure often isn't too hard to come by, even for busy leaner-inners—by the ends of our busy days, often we might feel like we have inadequate energy left to do anything but scroll or watch TV. You spend all your fucks for the day, and eventually you have no fucks left to give to anything but a screen. You can find me many evenings with eyes glazed over, soft clothes on, and a little drool dribbling from the corner of my mouth as I let my brain turn mostly off in front of a screen.

There's absolutely nothing wrong with passive leisure, and you should let yourself have plenty. Completely abolish the concept of "guilty pleasure" from your vocabulary.

> *Do you like some little TV show you know is dumb? Great! That's not a guilty pleasure, it's just a* <u>*pleasure.*</u>

Do you follow some influencer who you know is having a bad influence on you? Perfect! Let the influence wash over you, laugh, and move on.

But there is a more satisfying kind of leisure: active leisure. When most people imagine what they'd like to do with their spare time, they picture passive leisure: relaxing. But tap them on the shoulder while they're performing passive leisure—say, sitting in a comfy chair reading a book and sipping tea—and ask them how happy they are. The relaxing person tends to say they're medium happy. (And, let's get real, medium happy is pretty good.)

Tap someone on the shoulder while they're enjoying active leisure—hiking a trail they've never been on before, performing a song at an open mic night, volunteering time at a local social justice organization, sharing a bottle of wine with a friend—and they report much higher levels of satisfaction. What these activities have in common is that you have to plan to do them, and they sound a bit scary on their face.

> *Psychologists will tell you that the activities that intimidate us the most also make us the __happiest__.*

So, take your planner back out. If you have an hour of TV booked every day, then good: You're really reading carefully. But now you have to add more: activities that are a little outside your comfort zone, that get you out of your house, experiencing novel places or people or ideas.

Ultimately, you need something in your calendar—something you've already paid for, or that others are depending on you to do—to help you remember to actually have some fucking fun.

Solo Activities That Are Easy to Avoid	*Social* Activities You Just Can't Quit
Read a book	Join a book club and make a bunch of other people read the book you're reading and force them to talk to you about it.
Exercise	Join the rec league's Frisbee golf and/or pickleball clubs. Immediately start talking nonstop about how awesome Frisbee golf and/or pickleball are.
Learn a language	Find a language exchange partner to miscommunicate with. Then, when you get pretty good at the language, volunteer with an organization that services that language community, so that many people will witness you confusing the word for "dog" with the word for "husband."
Create art	Take an art class at the local community college. Proceed to give everyone you know handmade ashtrays as gifts even though they don't smoke, because they're the only kind of pottery you know how to make.

Change **More**

Before he was encouraging us, in his gentle soothing voice, to add a few happy little trees to our landscapes on PBS's *The Joy of Painting*, Bob Ross was a drill sergeant in the air force.)

I know this sounds made up, so I'll patiently wait while you google it.

For many of us, leaning in—achieving everything, striving for perfection at work and at home, equating our self-worth with what we've "accomplished," never giving ourselves a break—is less a choice we make than an apparently unavoidable situation we find ourselves in each day. Sometimes it feels like you started on a certain trajectory in life and once that train left the station there was no turning back.

My hope is that this book—and Bob Ross's striking career change—has proved that's not true. You don't need to break your neck leaning in. And it doesn't take much to change your trajectory.

Maybe you wake up one day and realize you're not a drill sergeant. You're an art teacher! But shit, you've already been drill sergeanting for so long, what are you going to do? Just fucking quit? And become, like, an art teacher?

Yes. The answer to that is, fucking yes.

My request that you "change more" doesn't have to mean upending your life, completely stopping your current trajectory, and taking up a wholly new path.

Start by microdosing leaning the fuck out.

See what happens if you don't cook dinner as many nights as you used to. So what if you don't respond to a so-called "urgent" work email at 11 p.m.? See whether the Earth crumbles if you care less what other people think of you.

After you make a couple of tiny subtractions, make a couple of tiny additions. Ask an old friend out for coffee. Go to an intriguing event one night, even if you're tired—something that's not related to your career or your kids or your "goals." Something frivolous as fuck.

Keep trying little changes, remaining conscious that you are choosing to lean the fuck out of a few demands, and instead let yourself enjoy a less stressful life.

Once you form the habit of saying no to overwork and internalized pressure, it starts to feel natural and intuitive to live a life balanced between obligations and whatever the fuck you want to do.

In other words, once you develop the habit of choosing enjoyment over achievement, the line between leaning in and leaning the fuck out disappears. You're not leaning in any direction at all.

You're just living.

Acknowledgments

It's not easy to write a book, especially while practicing the *Lean the F*ck Out* principles recommended in the very book you're writing. These people helped, and I owe them many thanks:

✩ For his intelligence, comfort, and humor, my husband, who does what every spouse of every woman should do to ensure she has enough time to write a book—namely, slightly more than half the parenting and household labor.

✩ For being curious, creative, sharp, and sweet, my kids, who think every time Mommy is at her computer and ignoring them it's because she's "checking work email," which is more or less accurate.

✩ For seeing a "joyful manifesto" where I could only see a screed, my editor, Aimee Chase, who has been a privilege to work with.

✩ For taking humor seriously, the faculty, staff, and students of Ursinus College, who have supported me no matter what direction my brain wants to take my writing.

✩ For their encouragement and love, my mother, father, sister, brother, friends, and extended family, who have helped me see what's possible and have cheered me on.

✩ For their generosity and fun, all the women in my life, who have shared their lives with me, one visit, one text, and one meal at a time.

I wrote this book to try to make each of you laugh, and to encourage you to go easy on yourself.